Twilio Cookbook

Over 60 easy-to-follow recipes ranging from walking you through key features of Twilio's API to building advanced telephony applications

Enjoy the book :)

Roger Stringer

[PACKT]
PUBLISHING

BIRMINGHAM - MUMBAI

Twilio Cookbook

First published: September 2013

Production Reference: 1300813

Published by Packt Publishing Ltd.
Livery Place
35 Livery Street
Birmingham B3 2PB, UK.

ISBN 978-1-78216-606-1

www.packtpub.com

Cover Image by Abhishek Pandey (abhishek.pandey1210@gmail.com)

Credits

Author
Roger Stringer

Reviewer
Jakir Hayder

Acquisition Editors
Rukhsana Khambatta
Sam Birch

Lead Technical Editor
Dayan Hyames

Technical Editors
Sharvari H. Baet
Jalasha D'costa
Dipika Gaonkar
Aparna Kumari

Copy Editors
Mradula Hegde
Gladson Monteiro
Aditya Nair
Laxmi Subramanian

Project Coordinator
Apeksha Chitnis

Proofreaders
Stephen Copestake
Maria Gould

Indexer
Hemangini Bari

Production Coordinator
Arvindkumar Gupta

Cover Work
Arvindkumar Gupta

About the Author

Roger Stringer has been a PHP developer since 2001 and has been working on projects of all sizes for companies all over the world. He has also formed several startups over the years and most of them have been powered by Twilio to provide services.

When not working on the Web, Roger can be found reading, cooking, and spending time with his daughter Kaitlyn at local farmers' markets.

Roger is the founder of The Interviewr, a Twilio-powered startup that makes interviewing more efficient by helping with scheduling, contact management, and conducting and recording interviews.

I'd like to thank my wife Patsy and our daughter Kaitlyn for having the patience to let me get this book written. There were many hours that I spent behind a computer typing.

Rob and the Twilio crew for answering any questions that came up as I worked on the various topics covered.

I also want to thank Jason and the crew at Copter Labs and Gary and the VeriCorder team.

About the Reviewer

Jakir Hayder graduated in Computer Science from South East University and is doing his MS in Computer Science and Engineering from North South University in Bangladesh. He has been building websites and social networking apps since 1999. He has been developing Facebook apps since 2007. He gave his talk at Facebook Developer Garage, Dhaka. He has developed websites with deep integration with Facebook, Twitter, LinkedIn, and YouTube APIs. He writes tests with RSpec, Cucumber, and Capybara with Selenium. He follows Agile methodologies of software development and is specially fond of scrum and standup.

Besides his full-time job, Jakir writes his blog at `blog.jambura.com`. He can be followed on Twitter `@jakirhayder` and on his LinkedIn profile `bd.linkedin.com/in/zakirhyder`. He lives in Bangladesh with his wife Fathema and his son Arham. Currently, Jakir is working as a Sr. Software Engineer at Cellbazaar, the biggest classified ads site in Bangladesh.

I'd like to thank my wife for taking care of my three-month old boy while I reviewed the book and did my job. I'd also like to thank Apeksha Chitnis for being patient with me.

www.PacktPub.com

Support files, eBooks, discount offers, and more

You might want to visit www.PacktPub.com for support files and downloads related to your book.

Did you know that Packt offers eBook versions of every book published, with PDF and ePub files available? You can upgrade to the eBook version at www.PacktPub.com and as a print book customer, you are entitled to a discount on the eBook copy. Get in touch with us at service@packtpub.com for more details.

At www.PacktPub.com, you can also read a collection of free technical articles, sign up for a range of free newsletters, and receive exclusive discounts and offers on Packt books and eBooks.

http://PacktLib.PacktPub.com

Do you need instant solutions to your IT questions? PacktLib is Packt's online digital book library. Here, you can access, read and search across Packt's entire library of books.

Why Subscribe?

- ► Fully searchable across every book published by Packt
- ► Copy and paste, print and bookmark content
- ► On-demand and accessible via web browsers

Free Access for Packt account holders

If you have an account with Packt at www.PacktPub.com, you can use this to access PacktLib today and view nine entirely free books. Simply use your login credentials for immediate access.

Table of Contents

Preface

Phones are everywhere! From calling to texting, you use phones for your business and for personal use. Twilio provides an API that lets you combine phone calls and SMS messages with your websites.

Twilio Cookbook will get you on the fast lane to learning how to use Twilio with PHP and MySQL to add phone and SMS services to your websites; you'll also rapidly learn how to set up systems such as a company directory, PBX, a voicemail system, an order-tracking system, and finally how to set up two-factor authentication.

What this book covers

Chapter 1, Into the Frying Pan, covers what you need to know about adding two-factor authentication to a website to verify users. This chapter helps you set up a basic order-verification system, add the Click-to-Call functionality to a website, and record phone calls. We will also set up a company directory and learn how to use Twilio Client for Text-to-Speech.

Chapter 2, Now We're Cooking, begins by covering how to create usage records and then proceeds to topics such as screen calls to be actually answered by a person, buying a phone number, setting up a voicemail system, and building an emergency calling system.

Chapter 3, Conducting Surveys via SMS, builds a system that lets you add subscribers, build a survey, send surveys to subscribers, and view responses that come back.

Chapter 4, Building a Conference Calling System, shows you how to build a handy conference calling system that includes scheduling, notifying attendees, recording the conference call, joining the call from a browser or from a phone, monitoring the conference, and muting attendees.

Chapter 5, Combining Twilio with Other APIs, shows you how to use Twilio with other APIs to add features such as a local business search via text messages, a movie listings search, and a weather look-up. You'll also learn how to search Google.

Chapter 6, Sending and Receiving SMS Messages, digs into the many SMS messaging features that Twilio provides, beginning with sending messages from a website to replying to messages from a phone, sending bulk SMS messages to a list of people, SMS order tracking to check on orders, serving a group chat platform, and sending SMS messages from a phone call.

Chapter 7, Building a Reminder System, uses Twilio's SMS services to let you schedule reminders, get notifications of the reminders set, retrieve a list of reminders, cancel a reminder, and add another person to a reminder.

Chapter 8, Building an IVR System, shows you how to set up an Interactive Voice Response system, beginning with a basic phone tree, screening and recording calls, logging and reporting calls, looking up contacts on incoming calls using the HighRiseHQ API, and sending SMS messages to www.Salesforce.com contacts.

Chapter 9, Building Your Own PBX, shows you how to set up subaccounts for each of your users, letting them buy their own phone numbers, accept incoming phone calls, make outgoing phone calls, and delete their accounts.

Chapter 10, Digging into OpenVBX, takes you into the world of building plugins for the OpenVBX system, starting with a call log plugin, going into a searchable company directory, collecting payments over the phone using Stripe, tracking orders, setting up a caller ID system, and testing call flows.

What you need for this book

All you need to get started is a Twilio account, a web host, a simple text editor such as Notepad++, Emacs, or Vim, and an Internet connection.

Who this book is for

This book is for programmers who have already used PHP and MySQL in one way or another. It's for people who work with a lot of backend code and want to get up to speed with the world of Twilio. It's for people who want to use the capabilities of Twilio to let their websites handle phone calls and SMS messages.

The book is for both beginners and seasoned developers and assumes that you have some experience in PHP and MySQL already. In-depth knowledge of these applications is not necessary, however.

Conventions

In this book, you will find a number of styles of text that distinguish between different kinds of information. Here are some examples of these styles, and an explanation of their meaning.

Code words in text are shown as follows: "Create a file called `search.php` in your `views` folder."

A block of code is set as follows:

```
<h3>Choose a Twilio number to buy</h3>
<?php   foreach($numbers->available_phone_numbers as $number){ ?>
  <form method="POST" action="<?=$uri?>/buy">
  <label><?php echo $number->friendly_name ?></label>
  <input type="hidden" name="PhoneNumber" value="<?php echo $number-
>phone_number ?>">
  <input type="hidden" name="action" value="buy" />
  <input type="submit" name="submit" value="BUY" />
  </form>
<?php   }   ?>
```

New terms and **important words** are shown in bold. Words that you see on the screen, in menus or dialog boxes for example, appear in the text like this: "We now have a menu option under the **Admin** menu called **Test Call Flow**."

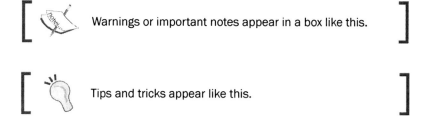

Warnings or important notes appear in a box like this.

Tips and tricks appear like this.

Reader feedback

Feedback from our readers is always welcome. Let us know what you think about this book—what you liked or may have disliked. Reader feedback is important for us to develop titles that you really get the most out of.

To send us general feedback, simply send an e-mail to `feedback@packtpub.com`, and mention the book title via the subject of your message.If there is a topic that you have expertise in and you are interested in either writing or contributing to a book, see our author guide on `www.packtpub.com/authors`.

Customer support

Now that you are the proud owner of a Packt book, we have a number of things to help you to get the most from your purchase.

Downloading the example code

You can download the example code files for all Packt books you have purchased from your account at `http://www.packtpub.com`. If you purchased this book elsewhere, you can visit `http://www.packtpub.com/support` and register to have the files e-mailed directly to you.

Errata

Although we have taken every care to ensure the accuracy of our content, mistakes do happen. If you find a mistake in one of our books—maybe a mistake in the text or the code—we would be grateful if you would report this to us. By doing so, you can save other readers from frustration and help us improve subsequent versions of this book. If you find any errata, please report them by visiting `http://www.packtpub.com/submit-errata`, selecting your book, clicking on the **errata submission form** link, and entering the details of your errata. Once your errata are verified, your submission will be accepted and the errata will be uploaded on our website, or added to any list of existing errata, under the Errata section of that title. Any existing errata can be viewed by selecting your title from `http://www.packtpub.com/support`.

Piracy

Piracy of copyright material on the Internet is an ongoing problem across all media. At Packt, we take the protection of our copyright and licenses very seriously. If you come across any illegal copies of our works, in any form, on the Internet, please provide us with the location address or website name immediately so that we can pursue a remedy.

Please contact us at `copyright@packtpub.com` with a link to the suspected pirated material.

We appreciate your help in protecting our authors, and our ability to bring you valuable content.

Questions

You can contact us at `questions@packtpub.com` if you are having a problem with any aspect of the book, and we will do our best to address it.

1
Into the Frying Pan

In this chapter we will cover:

- ▶ Adding two-factor voice authentication to verify users
- ▶ Using Twilio SMS to set up two-factor authentication for secure websites
- ▶ Adding order verification
- ▶ Adding Click-to-Call functionality to your website
- ▶ Recording a phone call
- ▶ Setting up a company directory
- ▶ Setting up Text-to-Speech

Introduction

Twilio's API allows you to do some incredible things. Combine it with PHP and you have a powerful tool that you can use to enhance your business or even build entirely new businesses around it.

I've worked with Twilio on dozens of projects over the past three and a half years and have built entire startups around it such as `TheInterviewr.com`.

This chapter will get you started on using Twilio for two-factor authentication functionality, order verification, adding Click-to-Call to your website, recording phone calls, setting up a company directory, and using Twilio Client to add Text-to-Speech capabilities to your website.

Before we begin, you'll need a twilio.com account, so go to `http://twilio.com` and sign up.

To get started, you will want to have Twilio's helper library at `http://www.twilio.com/docs/libraries`.

You can get your Twilio **ACCOUNT SID** and **AUTH TOKEN** from your account page here:

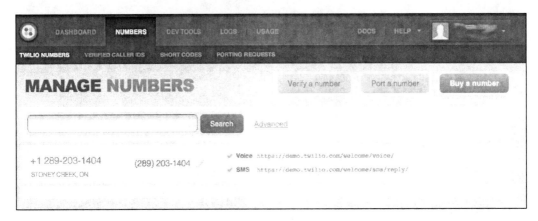

You can also click on **NUMBERS** to manage your list:

Now, let's get started with some code...

Adding two-factor voice authentication to verify users

Being able to verify that the users are actual users, and being able to help them have better security, is an important factor for everyone, and that's where two-factor authentication comes in handy.

Two-factor authentication is a more secure way of logging in to a website. In addition to entering a password online, a user has to enter a random verification code generated at login time. This combination of passwords makes it easier to safeguard your applications.

Two-factor authentication is used in:

- E-commerce sites
- Sites that allow users to sign up
- Recovering lost passwords (by sending the new code to a phone number already saved)

More and more big web services are starting to activate two-factor authentication as they realize how important it can be. Amazon, Google, and Apple are just some of the companies that have begun utilizing two-factor authentication for user protection.

Getting ready

The complete source code for this recipe can be found in at `Chapter1/Recipe1`.

How to do it...

We're going to build our first Twilio app, a two-factor voice authentication system. This can be plugged into websites to allow users to get called on a phone and verify whether they are who they say they are. Perform the following steps:

1. Download the Twilio Helper Library (from `https://github.com/twilio/twilio-php/zipball/master`) and unzip it.

2. Upload the `Services/` folder to your website.

3. Upload `config.php` to your website and make sure the following variables are set:

```php
<?php
  $accountsid = ''; //    YOUR TWILIO ACCOUNT SID
  $authtoken = '';  //    YOUR TWILIO AUTH TOKEN
  $fromNumber = ''; //    PHONE NUMBER CALLS WILL COME FROM
?>
```

This file will let you configure your web app with your Twilio account information.

4. We'll set up a file called `two-factor-voice.php`, which will sit on your web server. This file handles the two-factor authentication:

```php
<?php
  session_start();
  include 'Services/Twilio.php';
  include 'config.php';
  include 'functions.php';
  $username = cleanVar('username');
  $password = cleanVar('password');
  $phoneNum = cleanVar('phone_number');
  if( isset($_POST['action']) ){
    if( isset($_POST['username']) &&
      isset($_POST['phone_number'])
      ){
      $message = user_generate_token($username,
        $phoneNum,'calls');
    }else if( isset($_POST['username']) &&
      isset($_POST['password']) ){
      $message = user_login($username, $password);
    }
    header("Location: two-factor-voice.php?message=" .
      urlencode($message));
```

```
        exit;
    }
?>
<html>
<body>
  <p>Please enter a username, and a phone number you can be
     reached at, we will then call you with your one-time
     password</p>
  <span id="message">
  <?php
     echo cleanVar('message');
     $action = (isset($_SESSION['password'])) ? 'login' :
       'token';
  ?>
  </span>
  <form id="reset-form"  method="POST" class="center">
  <input type="hidden" name="action" value="<?php echo
     $action;
     ?>" />
  <p>Username: <input type="text" name="username"
     id="username"
     value="<?php echo $_SESSION['username']; ?>" /></p>
  <?php if (isset($_SESSION['password'])) { ?>
  <p>Password: <input type="password" name="password"
     id="password" /></p>
  <?php } else { ?>
  <p>Phone Number: <input type="text" name="phone_number"
     id="phone_number" /></p>
  <input type="hidden" name="method" value="voice" />
  <?php } ?>
  <p><input type="submit" name="submit" id="submit"
     value="login!"/></p>
  <p> </p>
  </form>
</body>
</html>
```

You may notice one of the functions we called is `cleanVar()`; this is a little function I like to use to make sure certain variables, specifically usernames, passwords, and phone numbers, follow a set rule.

5. Finally, create a file called `functions.php` on your web server:

```php
<?php
function cleanVar($key){
  $retVal = '';
  $retVal = isset( $_REQUEST[$key]) ?
    $_REQUEST[$key] : '';
  switch($key){
    case 'username':
    case 'password':
      $retVal = preg_replace("/[^A-Za-z0-9]/",
        "", $retVal);
      break;
    case 'phone_number':
      $retVal = preg_replace("/[^0-9]/", "", $retVal);
      break;
    case 'message':
      $retVal = urldecode($retVal);
      $retVal = preg_replace("/[^A-Za-z0-9 ,']/",
        "", $retVal);

  }
  return $retVal;
}


function user_generate_token($username, $phoneNum,
  $method='calls'){
  global $accountsid, $authtoken, $fromNumber;
  $password = substr(md5(time().rand(0, 10^10)), 0, 10);
  $_SESSION['username'] = $username;
  $_SESSION['password'] = $password;
  $client = new Services_Twilio($accountsid, $authtoken);
  $content = "Your newly generated password
    is ".$password."To repeat that, your password
    is ".$password;
  $item = $client->account->$method->create(
    $fromNumber,
    $phoneNum,
    $content
  );
  $message = "A new password has been generated and sent
    to your phone number.";
  return $message;
}
```

```
function user_login($username, $submitted) {
  // Retrieve the stored password
  $stored = $_SESSION['password'];
  // Compare the retrieved vs the stored password
  if ($stored == $submitted) {
    $message = "Hello and welcome back $username";
  }else {
    $message = "Sorry, that's an invalid username and
      password combination.";
  }
  // Clean up after ourselves
  unset($_SESSION['username']);
  unset($_SESSION['password']);
  return $message;
}
?>
```

How it works...

In steps 1 and 2, we downloaded and installed the Twilio Helper Library for PHP; this library is the heart of your Twilio-powered apps.

In step 3, we uploaded `config.php` that contains our authentication information to talk to Twilio's API.

When your users go to `two-factor-voice.php`, they are presented with a form where they enter a username and their phone number. Once they submit the form, it generates a one-time usage password and sends it as a text message to the phone number they entered. They then enter this password in the form on the site to verify that they are who they say they are.

I've used this on several different types of websites; it's a feature that people always want in some way to help verify that your users are who they say they are.

Using Twilio SMS to set up two-factor authentication for secure websites

This recipe is similar to the two-factor voice authentication recipe but uses SMS instead and texts the user their one-time password.

Again, two-factor authentication is an important tool to verify your users for various purposes and should be used on sites if you care at all about user security.

Forcing a user to verify their identity using two-factor authentication, in order to do something as simple as changing their password, can help promote trust between both you and your users.

Getting ready

The complete source code for this recipe can be found at `Chapter1/Recipe2`.

How to do it...

We're going to build our first Twilio app, a two-factor SMS authentication system. This can be plugged into websites to allow users to get called on a phone and verify that they are who they say they are.

1. Download the Twilio Helper Library (from `https://github.com/twilio/twilio-php/zipball/master`) and unzip it.

2. Upload the `Services/` folder to your website.

3. Upload `config.php` to your website and make sure the following variables are set:

```php
<?php
  $accountsid = '';  //  YOUR TWILIO ACCOUNT SID
  $authtoken = '';   //      YOUR TWILIO AUTH TOKEN
  $fromNumber = '';  //  PHONE NUMBER CALLS WILL COME FROM
?>
```

4. We'll set up a file called `two-factor-sms.php`, which will sit on your web server; this file handles the two-factor authentication.

```php
<?php
  session_start();
  include 'Services/Twilio.php';
  include 'config.php';
  include 'functions.php';
  $username = cleanVar('username');
  $password = cleanVar('password');
  $phoneNum = cleanVar('phone_number');
  if( isset($_POST['action']) ){
    if( isset($_POST['username']) &&
      isset($_POST['phone_number'])){
        $message = user_generate_token($username, $phoneNum,
          'sms');
  }else if( isset($_POST['username']) &&
    isset($_POST['password'])
    ){
    $message = user_login($username, $password);
  }
  header("Location: two-factor-sms.php?message=" .
    urlencode($message));
```

```
    exit;
  }
  ?>
  <html>
  <body>
  <p>Please enter a username, and a phone number you can be reached
  at, we will then send you your one-time password via SMS.</p>
  <span id="message">
  <?php
    echo cleanVar('message');
    $action = (isset($_SESSION['password'])) ? 'login' : 'token';
  ?>
  </span>
  <form id="reset-form"  method="POST" class="center">
  <input type="hidden" name="action" value="<?php echo
    $action; ?>"/>
  <p>Username: <input type="text" name="username"
    id="username" value="<?php echo $_SESSION['username'];
    ?>" /></p>
  <?php if (isset($_SESSION['password'])) { ?>
    <p>Password: <input type="password" name="password"
      id="password" /></p>
  <?php } else { ?>
    <p>Phone Number: <input type="text" name="phone_number"
      id="phone_number" /></p>
    <input type="hidden" name="method" value="sms" checked="checked"
      />
  <?php } ?>
  <p><input type="submit" name="submit" id="submit"
    value="login!"/></p>
  <p> </p>
  </form>
  </body>
  </html>
```

5. Finally, we're going to include the same functions.php file we used in the *Adding two-factor voice authentication to verify users* recipe.

How it works...

In steps 1 and 2, we downloaded and installed the Twilio Helper Library for PHP; this library is the heart of your Twilio-powered apps.

In step 3, we uploaded config.php that contains our authentication information to talk to Twilio's API.

Your user is presented with a form where they enter a username and their phone number. Once they submit the form, it generates a one-time usage password and sends it as a text message to the phone number they entered. They then enter this password in the form on the site to verify that they are who they say they are.

What's the big difference between recipes 1 and 2? Really, it's that one does voice and one does SMS. You could combine these as options if you wanted to so that people can choose between voice or SMS. The biggest key is when you call the function `user_generate_token`; you specify the method as either `calls` or `sms`.

Adding order verification

If you handle any type of commerce, such as e-commerce and callin orders, you know that giving your customers a way to quickly check their orders is handy for selling anything.

Making things easy for customers keeps them coming back again; having a way for your customers to just text you an order ID and tracking their purchase at any time is really handy.

In this example, a user will text an order ID and we will return a result based on an array.

The array will be formatted by order ID and status as follows:

```
$orders = array(
   'order id'=>'status'
);
```

Getting ready

The complete source code for this recipe can be found at `Chapter1/Recipe3`.

How to do it...

We're going to set up a simple order verification system. A user will text us an order number and we will reply back with the status of that order.

1. Upload a file called `order_verification.php` to your server:

```php
<?php
$orders = array(
   '111'=>'shipped',
   '222'=>'processing',
   '333'=>'awaiting fullfillment'
);
if( isset($_POST['Body']) ){
   $phone = $_POST['From'];
   $order_id = strtolower($_POST['Body']);
```

```
    $status = order_lookup($order_id);
    print_sms_reply("Your order is currently set at
      status'".$status."'");
  }else{
    print_sms_reply("Please send us your order id and we
      will look it up ASAP");
  }
  function print_sms_reply ($sms_reply){
    echo "<?xml version=\"1.0\" encoding=\"UTF-8\"?>\n";
    echo "<Response>\n<Sms>\n";
    echo $sms_reply;
    echo "</Sms></Response>\n";
  }
  function order_lookup($order_id){
    global $orders;
    if( isset($orders[$order_id]) ){
      return $orders[$order_id];
    }
    return 'No Order Matching that ID was found';
  }
?>
```

2. To have a number point to this script, log in to your Twilio account and point your Twilio phone number to it:

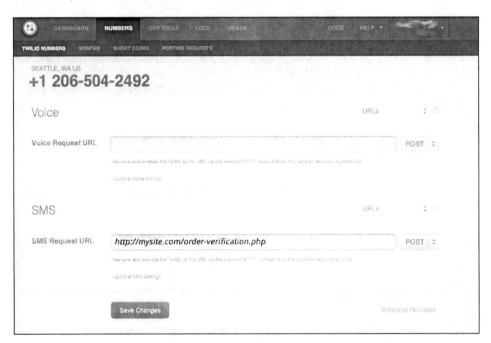

Insert the URL in the **SMS Request URL** field on this page. Then, any text messages that you receive on this number will be processed via `order_verification.php`.

How it works...

In step 1, we created `order_verification.php`.

In step 2, we configured a number in our Twilio account to call `order_verification.php`.

This is a one-step recipe. A user sends you a text message containing their order ID; you then perform a lookup and return the status.

If no order exists, it returns that the order wasn't found in the system.

Adding the Click-to-Call functionality to your website

Click-to-Call is a handy functionality where you can have your website visitors click a button to start a call. This can be useful for handling support, sales calls, or just chatting with your users.

Getting ready

The complete source code for this recipe can be found at `Chapter1/Recipe4`.

How to do it...

Ready? We're going to build a simple Click-to-Call system. With this, you can set up any website to allow a visitor to type in a phone number and connect a call between you and them.

1. Download the Twilio Helper Library (from `https://github.com/twilio/twilio-php/zipball/master`) and unzip it.

2. Upload the `Services/` folder to your website.

3. Upload `config.php` to your website and make sure the following variables are set:
    ```php
    <?php
      $accountsid = '';  //   YOUR TWILIO ACCOUNT SID
      $authtoken = '';  //      YOUR TWILIO AUTH TOKEN
      $fromNumber = '';  //   PHONE NUMBER CALLS WILL COME FROM
      $toNumber = '';  //   YOUR PHONE NUMBER TO CONNECT TO
    ?>
    ```

4. Upload a file called `click-to-call.php` to your website:

```php
<?php
session_start();
include 'Services/Twilio.php';
include("config.php");
if( isset($_GET['msg']) )
  echo $msg;
?>
<h3>Please enter your phone number, and you will be
  connected to <?=$toNumber?></h3>
<form action="makecall.php" method="post">
<span>Your Number: <input type="text" name="called"
 /></span>
<input type="submit" value="Connect me!" />
</form>
```

This file displays a form that, when submitted, triggers the rest of the calling process.

5. Now, upload a file named `makecall.php` to your website:

```php
<?php
session_start();
include 'Services/Twilio.php';
include("config.php");

$client = new Services_Twilio($accountsid, $authtoken);
if (!isset($_REQUEST['called'])) {
  $err = urlencode("Must specify your phone number");
  header("Location: click-to-call.php?msg=$err");
  die;
}
$call = $client->account->calls->create($fromNumber,
  $toNumber,
  'callback.php?number=' . $_REQUEST['called']);
$msg = urlencode("Connecting... ".$call->sid);
header("Location: click-to-call.php?msg=$msg");
?>
```

6. Finally, upload a file named `callback.php` to your website:

```php
<?php
  header("content-type: text/xml");
  echo "<?xml version=\"1.0\" encoding=\"UTF-8\"?>\n";
?>
<Response>
```

```
<Say>A customer at the number <?php echo
  $_REQUEST['number']?>
  is calling</Say>
<Dial><?php echo $_REQUEST['number']?></Dial>
</Response>
```

How it works...

In steps 1 and 2, we downloaded and installed the Twilio Helper Library for PHP.

In step 3, we uploaded `config.php` containing our authentication information to talk to Twilio's API.

In steps 4, 5, and 6, we created the backbone of our Click-to-Call system.

We display a form on your website, where a user enters his or her phone number and clicks the **Connect me!** button. The system then calls your phone number; once you answer, it will connect you to the user.

Recording a phone call

Recording a call is handy for conducting interviews. In this example, we're going to build on the Click-to-Call recipe and add in the ability to record the call.

Getting ready

The complete source code for this recipe can be found at `Chapter1/Recipe5`.

How to do it...

This recipe will expand on our Click-to-Call system to include the ability to record the phone call. We'll also set up a nice method to retrieve recordings.

1. Download the Twilio Helper Library (from `https://github.com/twilio/twilio-php/zipball/master`) and unzip it.
2. Upload the `Services/` folder to your website.
3. Upload `config.php` to your website and make sure the following variables are set:

```php
<?php
  $accountsid = '';  //  YOUR TWILIO ACCOUNT SID
  $authtoken = '';  //  YOUR TWILIO AUTH TOKEN
  $fromNumber = '';  //  PHONE NUMBER CALLS WILL COME FROM
  $toNumber = '';  //      YOUR PHONE NUMBER TO CONNECT TO
  $toEmail = '';  // YOUR EMAIL ADDRESS TO SEND RECORDING TO
?>
```

4. Upload a file called `record-call.php` to your website:

```php
<?php
session_start();
include 'Services/Twilio.php';
include("config.php");
if( isset($_GET['msg']) )
  echo $msg;
?>
<h3>Please enter your phone number, and you will be
  connected to <?=$toNumber?></h3>
<form action="makecall.php" method="post">
<span>Your Number: <input type="text"
  name="called" /></span>
<input type="submit" value="Connect me!" />
</form>
```

This file displays a form that, when submitted, triggers the rest of the calling process.

5. Now, upload a file named `makecall.php` to your website:

```php
<?php
session_start();
include 'Services/Twilio.php';
include("config.php");
$client = new Services_Twilio($accountsid, $authtoken);
if (!isset($_REQUEST['called'])) {
  $err = urlencode("Must specify your phone number");
  header("Location: record-call.php?msg=$err");
  die;
}

$url = (!empty($_SERVER['HTTPS'])) ?
"https://".$_SERVER['SERVER_NAME'].$_SERVER['REQUEST_URI'] :
"http://".$_SERVER['SERVER_NAME'].$_SERVER['REQUEST_URI'];
$url = str_replace("makecall","recording",$url);

$call = $client->account->calls->create($fromNumber, $to,
  'callback.php?number=' .
  $_REQUEST['called'],array("record"=>true));

$msg = urlencode("Connecting... ".$call->sid);
$_SESSION['csid'] = $call->sid;
$RecordingUrl = $url."?csid=".$call->sid;
$subject = "New phone recording from
  {$_REQUEST['called']}";
```

```php
$body = "You have a new phone recording from
  {$_REQUEST['called']}:\n\n";

$body .= $RecordingUrl;

$headers = 'From: noreply@'.$_SERVER['SERVER_NAME']
  . "\r\n" .
  'Reply-To: noreply@'.$_SERVER['SERVER_NAME'] . "\r\n" .
  'X-Mailer: Twilio';
mail($toEmail, $subject, $body, $headers);
header("Location: record-call.php?msg=$msg");
?>
```

The `makecall.php` file handles the actual setting up of the call and also sends you an e-mail that provides you with a link to view the recording.

6. Next, upload a file named `callback.php` to your website:

```php
<?php
  header("content-type: text/xml");
  echo "<?xml version=\"1.0\" encoding=\"UTF-8\"?>\n";
?>
<Response>
  <Say>A customer at the number <?php echo
    $_REQUEST['number']?> is calling</Say>
  <Dial record=true><?php echo $_REQUEST['number']?></Dial>
</Response>
```

Did you catch what we did here? We told the `Dial` command to record the call. This means anything that is spoken during this call is now recorded.

7. Finally, upload a file named `recording.php` to your website:

```php
<?php
if( isset($_GET['csid']) ){
  getRecording( $_GET['csid'] );
}else{
  die( "Invalid recording!");
}
function getRecording($caSID){
  global $accountsid,$authtoken;
    $version = '2010-04-01';
    $url = "https://api.twilio.com/2010-04-
      01/Accounts/{$accountsid}/
      Calls/{$caSID}/Recordings.xml";
    $ch = curl_init();
    curl_setopt($ch, CURLOPT_URL, $url);
    curl_setopt($ch, CURLOPT_RETURNTRANSFER, true);
```

```
curl_setopt($ch, CURLOPT_USERPWD,
  "{$accountsid}:{$authtoken}");
curl_setopt($ch, CURLOPT_HTTPAUTH, CURLAUTH_BASIC);
$output = curl_exec($ch);
$info = curl_getinfo($ch);
curl_close($ch);
$output = simplexml_load_string($output);
echo "<table>";
foreach ($output->Recordings->Recording as $recording)
{
  echo "<tr>";
  echo "<td>".$recording->Duration." seconds</td>";
  echo "<td>".$recording->DateCreated."</td>";
  echo '<td><audio src="https://api.twilio.com/
    2010-04-01/Accounts/'.$sid.'/Recordings/
    '.$recording->Sid.'.mp3" controls preload="auto"
    autobuffer></audio></td>';
  echo "</tr>";
}
echo "</table>";
}
```

How it works...

In steps 1 and 2, we downloaded and installed the Twilio Helper Library for PHP.

In step 3, we uploaded config.php that contains our authentication information to talk to Twilio's API.

In steps 4, 5, and 6, we re-created the Click-to-Call functionality from the previous recipe but with one difference: we also set makecall.php to e-mail us a link to do the recording, as well as setting callback.php to actually do the recording.

As with the preceding *Adding Click-to-Call functionality to your website* recipe, a user is presented with a form on the website where they enter their information and click to begin a call. The difference here is that the call is actually recorded; once it's finished, the system e-mails you a link to listen to your recording.

One thing to remember with recordings is that it could take a few minutes after the call for the recording to be available. Hence, the script e-mails you a link to view the recording instead of the recording itself.

Setting up a company directory

A company directory is a very handy thing to have when you want a company phone number to be published and then have it contact other people in your company. It's also nice to make it searchable and that is what we are doing today.

This particular company directory has served me well at several companies I've worked with over the years and I'm especially pleased with its ability to convert names into their matching digits on a phone pad using this function:

```php
function stringToDigits($str) {
  $str = strtolower($str);
  $from = 'abcdefghijklmnopqrstuvwxyz';
  $to = '22233344455566677778889999';
  return preg_replace('/[^0-9]/', '', strtr($str, $from, $to));
}
```

This function works such that a name such as `Stringer` (my last name), gets converted into `78746437`. Then, as the caller does a search, it will return an employee whose name matches the digits entered and will then connect the call.

Getting ready

The complete source code for this recipe can be found at `Chapter1/Recipe6`.

How to do it...

We're going to build a basic, searchable company directory that will let callers either enter an extension or search by their last name.

1. Download the Twilio Helper Library (from `https://github.com/twilio/twilio-php/zipball/master`) and unzip it.

2. Upload the `Services/` folder to your website.

3. Upload `config.php` to your website and make sure the following variables are set:
   ```php
   <?php
     $accountsid = '';  //  YOUR TWILIO ACCOUNT SID
     $authtoken = '';  //  YOUR TWILIO AUTH TOKEN
     $fromNumber = '';  //  PHONE NUMBER CALLS WILL COME FROM
   ?>
   ```

4. Let's create the file called `company-directory-map.php`, which sets up the map for the company directory:

```php
<?php
  $directory = array(
    '0'=> array(
      'phone'=>'415-555-1111',
      'firstname' => 'John',
      'lastname' => 'Smith'
    ),
    '1234'=> array(
      'phone'=>'415-555-2222',
      'firstname' => 'Joe',
      'lastname' => 'Doe'
    ),
    '4321'=> array(
      'phone'=>'415-555-3333',
      'firstname' => 'Eric',
      'lastname' => 'Anderson'
    ),
  );
  $indexes = array();
  foreach($directory as $k=>$row){
    $digits = stringToDigits( $row['lastname'] );
    $indexes[ $digits] = $k;
  }
  function stringToDigits($str) {
    $str = strtolower($str);
    $from = 'abcdefghijklmnopqrstuvwxyz';
    $to = '22233344455566677778889999';
    return preg_replace('/[^0-9]/', '', strtr($str, $from,
      $to));
  }
  function getPhoneNumberByExtension($ext){
    global $directory;
    if( isset( $directory[$ext] ) ){
      return $directory[$ext];
    }
    return false;
  }
  function getPhoneNumberByDigits($digits){
    global $directory,$indexes;
    $search = false;
    foreach( $indexes as $i=>$ext ){
      if( stristr($i,$digits) ){
        $line = $directory[ $ext ];
        $search = array();
```

```php
            $search['name']= $line['firstname']."
               ".$line['lastname'];
            $search['extension']=$ext;
         }
      }
      return $search;
   }
?>
```

This file handles the list of extensions, and also takes care of the functions that handle the searching. One of the steps it performs is to loop through each extension and convert the last name into digits corresponding with a phone pad.

5. Now, we'll create `company-directory.php` to handle the logic for incoming calls:

```php
<?php
   session_start();
   include 'Services/Twilio.php';
   include 'config.php';
   include('company-directory-map.php');
   $first = true;
   if (isset($_REQUEST['Digits'])) {
      $digits = $_REQUEST['Digits'];
      if( $digits == "*"){
         header("Location: company-directory-lookup?
            Digits=".$digits);
         exit();
      }
   } else {
      $digits='';
   }
   if( strlen($digits) ){
      $first = false;
      $phone_number = getPhoneNumberByExtension($digits);
      if($phone_number!=null){
         $r = new Services_Twilio_Twiml();
         $r->say("Thank you, dialing now");
         $r->dial($phone_number);
         header ("Content-Type:text/xml");
         print $r;
         exit();
      }
   }
   $r = new Services_Twilio_Twiml();
   $g = $r->gather();
   if($first){
      $g->say("Thank you for calling our company.");
   }else{
```

```php
  $g->say('I\'m sorry, we could not find the extension '
    . $_REQUEST['Digits']);
}
$g->say(" If you know your party's extension, please
  enter the extension now, followed by the pound sign.
  To search the directory, press star. Otherwise, stay on
  the line for the receptionist.");
$r->say("Connecting you to the operator, please stay on
  the line.");
$r->dial($receptionist_phone_number);
header ("Content-Type:text/xml");
print $r;
exit;
?>
```

All incoming calls will first come into this file and, from there, will either be redirected straight to an extension or start the lookup process based on the last name.

6. And finally, we create `company-directory-lookup.php` that adds the ability to perform search operations:

```php
<?php
session_start();
include 'Services/Twilio.php';
include 'config.php';
include('company-directory-map.php');
$error = false;
if (isset($_REQUEST['Digits'])){
  $digits = $_REQUEST['Digits'];
}else{
  $digits='';
}
if(strlen($digits)){
  $result = getPhoneNumberByDigits($digits);
  if($result != false){
    $number = getPhoneNumberByExtension
      ($result['extension']);
    $r = new Services_Twilio_Twiml();
    $r->say($result['name']."'s extension is
      ".$result['extension']." Connecting you now");
    $r->dial($number);
    header ("Content-Type:text/xml");
    print $r;
    exit();
  } else {
    $error=true;
  }
}
```

```
$r = new Services_Twilio_Twiml();
if($error) $r->say("No match found for $digits");
$g = $r->gather();
$g->say("Enter the first four digits of the last name of
  the party you wish to reach, followed by the pound
  sign");
$r->say("I did not receive a response from you");
$r->redirect("company-directory.php");
header ("Content-Type:text/xml");
print $r;
?>
```

This file handles our lookups; as a caller types digits into a phone dial pad, this script will loop through the extensions to find a name that matches the digits entered.

7. Finally, we need to have a number point to this script. Upload `company-directory.php` somewhere and then point your Twilio phone number to it:

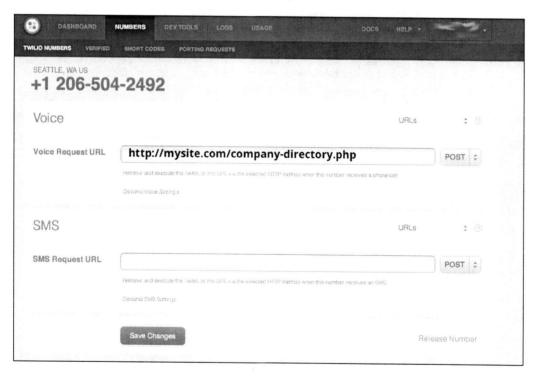

Insert the URL in the **Voice Request URL** field on this page. Then, any calls that you receive at this number will be processed via `company-directory.php`.

How it works...

In steps 1 and 2, we downloaded and installed the Twilio Helper Library for PHP.

In step 3, we uploaded `config.php` that contains our authentication information to talk to Twilio's API.

In step 4, we set up the `$directory` array in `company-directory-map.php`, which is the core of this system; it handles the extension number for each employee as well as containing his/her phone number, first name, and last name.

When a caller chooses to search for an employee, the last name is converted into corresponding digits similar to what you see on a phone.

So for example, `Stringer` becomes `78746437`; as the caller does a search, it will return an employee whose name matches and will then connect the call.

Finally, in step 7, we set up our phone number in Twilio to point to the location where `company-directory.php` has been uploaded so that all calls to that phone number go straight to `company-directory.php`.

You now have a nice, searchable company directory. I've been using this directory myself for the last two years at various companies and it works nicely.

Setting up Text-to-Speech

The final recipe of this chapter is going to use the Twilio Client to add handy functionality on your site.

Text-to-Speech is useful for having a voice read back text on a web page. You could do this by having a textbox of text that gets read back; or maybe you want to select text on a web page to be read back to a visitor.

Twilio Client is also handy for doing phone work straight from your browser.

Getting ready

The complete source code for this recipe can be found at `Chapter1/Recipe7`.

How to do it...

We're going to use the Twilio Client to set up a form where people can type in a message and have it spoken back to them either by a male or female voice.

1. First, since this is using the Twilio Client, you need to set up a Twiml app under your account.

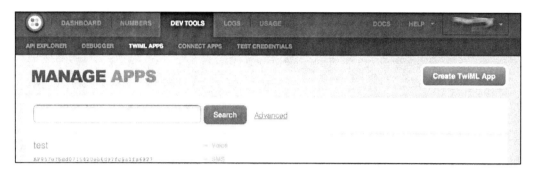

Click on the **Create TwiML App** button and enter a name for your app. Also, you'll need to enter a URL for the **Voice**. In this case, set it to the URL where you have uploaded `incoming_call.php`, that is, `http://MYWEBSITE.COM/incoming_call.php`.

Now, go back to the application list and you will see your new app. Look at the line directly beneath the name of your app; this is your app SID. Copy that as you will need it for this recipe.

2. Download the Twilio Helper Library from `https://github.com/twilio/twilio-php/zipball/master` and unzip it.

3. Upload the `Services/` folder to your website.

4. Upload `config.php` to your website and make sure the following variables are set:

```php
<?php
  $accountsid = '';  //  YOUR TWILIO ACCOUNT SID
  $authtoken = '';   //       YOUR TWILIO AUTH TOKEN
  $fromNumber = '';  //  PHONE NUMBER CALLS WILL COME FROM
?>
```

5. Let's create a file on your website called `text-to-speech.php`:

```php
<?php
  require_once('Services/Twilio/Capability.php');
  include("config.php");
  $APP_SID = 'YOUR APP SID';
  $token = new Services_Twilio_Capability($accountsid,
    $authtoken);
  $token->allowClientOutgoing($APP_SID);
?>
<html>
<head>
  <title>Text-To-Speech</title>
  <script type="text/javascript" src=
    "https://ajax.googleapis.com/ajax/libs/jquery/
    1.6.2/jquery.min.js"></script>
  <script type="text/javascript"
    src="//static.twilio.com/libs/twiliojs/1.1/
    twilio.min.js"></script>
  <script type="text/javascript">
```

```
    Twilio.Device.setup("<?php echo $token-
      >generateToken();?>",{"debug":true});
    $(document).ready(function() {
      $("#submit").click(function() {
        speak();
      });
    });
    function speak() {
      var dialogue = $("#dialogue").val();
      var voice =
        $('input:radio[name=voice]:checked').val();
      $('#submit').attr('disabled', 'disabled');
      Twilio.Device.connect({ 'dialogue' :
        dialogue, 'voice' : voice });
    }
    Twilio.Device.disconnect(function (conn) {
      $('#submit').removeAttr('disabled');
    });
  </script>
</head>
<body>
<p>
  <label for="dialogue">Text to be spoken</label>
  <input type="text" id="dialogue" name="dialogue"
    size="50">
</p>
<p>
  <label for="voice-male">Male Voice</label>
  <input type="radio" id="voice-male" name="voice"
    value="1" checked="checked">
  <label for="voice-female">Female Voice</label>
  <input type="radio" id="voice-female" name="voice"
    value="2">
</p>
<p>
  <input type="button" id="submit" name="submit"
    value="Speak to me">
</p>
</body>
</html>
```

6. Now, let's create another file on your website called incoming_call.php, which is the file Twilio Client will call. This will then read back the text you entered using either a male or female voice:

```php
<?php
  header('Content-type: text/xml');
  echo '<?xml version="1.0" encoding="UTF-8" ?>';
  $dialogue = trim($_REQUEST['dialogue']);
  $voice = (int) $_REQUEST['voice'];
  if (strlen($dialogue) == 0){
  $dialogue = 'Please enter some text to be spoken.';
  }
if ($voice == 1){
  $gender = 'man';
}else {
  $gender = 'woman';
}
?>
<Response>
  <Say voice="<?php echo $gender; ?>"><?php echo
    htmlspecialchars($dialogue); ?></Say>
</Response>
```

How it works...

In step 1, we set up our Twiml app in our Twilio account.

In steps 2 and 3, we downloaded and installed the Twilio Helper Library for PHP.

In step 4, we uploaded config.php that contains our authentication information to talk to Twilio's API.

Using Twilio Client, this recipe will read the content of a text box and play it back to you in either a male or female voice.

Twilio Client is a nice addition to the Twilio API that lets you do phone work straight from the browser. This way, you can add functionality directly to your web apps.

2
Now We're Cooking

In this chapter we will cover the following:

- ▸ Tracking account usage
- ▸ Screening calls
- ▸ Buying a phone number
- ▸ Setting up a voicemail system
- ▸ Building an emergency calling system

Introduction

In *Chapter 1, Into the Frying Pan*, we brought to you some handy recipes for Twilio; we're going to continue that in this chapter.

First, we'll show you how to generate usage records that come in handy for tracking usage across your Twilio account, especially when you have a web app that has customers using it daily.

Call screening lets you check calls that are actually answered by a person; if a machine answers, we move on to the next phone number.

Buying a phone number is also handy when you have multiple users and want to let them purchase a phone number to use for their own account.

A voicemail system lets you give callers a voice mailbox to store messages in and then sends you an e-mail with the transcribed message.

Finally, the emergency calling system will try a list of phone numbers when you find yourself in an emergency situation, to find someone who answers.

Tracking account usage

Tracking your call usage is important if you handle a lot of calls or if you have a site that has multiple users.

My website, `theinterviewr.com`, looks through hundreds of calls being made each week; this call usage tracking helps me know which users are making which calls so that I can see who's heavily using the network and who is not.

This also helps me analyze things and make sure I'm actually charging users reasonably per call.

Getting ready

The complete source code for this recipe can be found in the `Chapter2/Recipe1` folder in the code bundle available at `www.packtpub.com/support`.

How to do it...

We're going to build a usage tracking system now to let us look at how our Twilio account is being used. Perform the following steps to do so:

1. Download the Twilio Helper Library from `https://github.com/twilio/twilio-php/zipball/master` and unzip it.

2. Upload the `Services/` folder to your website.

3. Upload `config.php` to your website and make sure the following variables are set:

```php
<?php
  $accountsid = '';  //   YOUR TWILIO ACCOUNT SID
  $authtoken = '';  //   YOUR TWILIO AUTH TOKEN
  $fromNumber = '';  //   PHONE NUMBER CALLS WILL COME FROM
?>
```

4. Create a file called `functions.php` with the following content:

```php
<?php
function get_usage( $action ){
  global $accountsid;
  $results = array();
  $fields = array();
  $url = "https://api.twilio.com/2010-04-01/Accounts/
{$accountsid}/Usage/Records";
  switch($action){
    case 'lm':  //   last month
        $url = $url."/LastMonth.json";
```

```php
        break;
      case 'custom':
        $startd = $_GET['startd'];
        $endd = $_GET['endd'];
        $startd = date('Y-m-d',strtotime($startd));
        $endd = date('Y-m-d',strtotime($endd));
          $url = $url."/Daily.json";
        $fields = array(
          "Category"=>'calls-inbound',
          "StartDate"=>$startd,
          "EndDate"=>$endd
        );
        break;
      case 'all':
          $url = $url.".json";
        break;
      case 'today':
      default:
        $url = $url."/Today.json";
        break;
  }
  if ( isset($url) ){
      $ch = curl_init();
      curl_setopt($ch, CURLOPT_URL, $url);
      curl_setopt($ch, CURLOPT_RETURNTRANSFER, true);
      curl_setopt($ch, CURLOPT_USERPWD,
"{$accountsid}:{$authtoken}");
      curl_setopt($ch, CURLOPT_HTTPAUTH, CURLAUTH_BASIC);
      if( count($fields) > 0 ){
    foreach($fields as $key=>$value) { $fields_string .=
$key.'='.$value.'&'; }
    rtrim($fields_string,'&');
          curl_setopt($ch,CURLOPT_POST,count($fields));
          curl_setopt($ch,CURLOPT_POSTFIELDS,$fields_string);
        }
      $results = curl_exec($ch);
      $info = curl_getinfo($ch);
      curl_close($ch);
      return json_decode( $results );
  }
  return array();
}
```

functions.php is the file that actually handles communicating with Twilio and returning the usage information.

5. Create a file on your website called call-usage.php, with the following code:

```php
<?php
  session_start();
  include 'Services/Twilio.php';
  include("config.php");
  include("functions.php");

  $client = new Services_Twilio($accountsid, $authtoken);

  $action = isset($_GET['action']) ? $_GET['action'] : 'today';
?>
  <nav>
    <a href="call-usage.php?action=today">Today</a>
    <a href="call-usage.php?action=lm">Last Month</a>
    <a href="call-usage.php?action=all">All Calls</a>
    <span>Custom Report:</span>
    <form action="" method="GET">
      <input type="hidden" name="action" value="custom" />
      <input type="date" name="startd" placeholder="Start Date" />
      <input type="date" name="endd" placeholder="End Date" />
      <button type="submit">Generate</button>
    </form>
  </nav>
  <hr />
<?php
  $results = get_usage($action){

  if( count($results > 0) ){
#    echo '<pre>'.print_r($results,true).'</pre>';
?>
    <table width=100%>
    <thead>
    <tr>
      <th>Category</th>
      <th>Description</th>
      <th>SID</th>
      <th>Start Date</th>
      <th>End Date</th>
      <th>Usage</th>
      <th>Usage Unit</th>
```

```php
      <th>Price</th>
      <th>Price Unit</th>
    </tr>
    </thead>
    <tbody>
<?php  foreach( $results->usage_records as $row ){  ?>
    <tr>
      <td><?= $row->category?></td>
      <td><?= $row->description?></td>
      <th><?= $row->account_sid?></th>
      <td><?= $row->start_date?></td>
      <td><?= $row->end_date?></td>
      <td><?= $row->usage?></td>
      <td><?= $row->usage_unit?></td>
      <td><?= $row->price?></td>
      <td><?= $row->price_unit?></td>
    </tr>
<?php    }  ?>
    </tbody>
    </table>
<?php
  }
?>
```

How it works...

In steps 1 and 2, we downloaded and installed the Twilio Helper Library for PHP. This library is at the heart of your Twilio-powered apps.

In step 3, we uploaded `config.php`, which contains our authentication information to communicate with Twilio's API.

In step 4, we uploaded `functions.php`, which includes the `function get_usage.php` file; this function takes your account ID, as well as the criteria you chose to search by, and returns a JSON-encoded document from Twilio.

We then display the usage logs on the site to view. This usage tracker displays the account that performed the call, the number of minutes, and the cost for the call. If you use subaccounts, it is handy for knowing what to bill your users each month.

This recipe also displays reports as per the present day, past week, past month, and also custom dates. This works well for getting an idea of how much usage you actually have.

Screening calls

Call screening is a useful ability to have on your calling systems. For example, let's say you have three people on call in your support department and you want to call the first available agent.

This recipe will try and connect to each phone number available in a given array and check to see if a person answers or not; if a person does, it connects the call.

Getting ready

The complete source code for this recipe can be found in the `Chapter2/Recipe2` folder.

How to do it...

We're going to build a call-handling system that will forward calls to our list of agents; the first agent who accepts the call by pushing a button will get the call.

1. Download the Twilio Helper Library from `https://github.com/twilio/twilio-php/zipball/master` and unzip it.

2. Upload the `Services/` folder to your website.

3. Upload `config.php` to your website and make sure the following variables are set:

```php
<?php
  $accountsid = '';   //   YOUR TWILIO ACCOUNT SID
  $authtoken = '';    //      YOUR TWILIO AUTH TOKEN
  $fromNumber = '';   //   PHONE NUMBER CALLS WILL COME FROM
?>
```

4. The call-screening feature we are building will consist of three files. The first file is called `call-screening.php` and contains the following code:

```php
<?php
$numbers = array("1234567890", "1234567891", "1234567892");
$number_index = isset($_REQUEST['number_index']) ? $_
REQUEST['number_index'] : "0";
$DialCallStatus = isset($_REQUEST['DialCallStatus']) ? $_
REQUEST['DialCallStatus'] : "";
header("content-type: text/xml");
```

```php
if($DialCallStatus!="completed" && $number_index<count($numbers)){
?>
  <Response>
    <Dial action="call-screening.php?number_index=<?php echo
$number_index+1 ?>">
    <Number url="areyouhuman.xml">
      <?php echo $numbers[$number_index] ?>
    </Number>
    </Dial>
  </Response>
<?php
} else {
?>
  <Response>
    <Hangup/>
  </Response>
<?php
}
?>
```

5. When the phone is answered, we trigger a call to `areyouhuman.xml` that prompts the person answering the phone to press any key. Pressing any key will notify the system that it is indeed a person.

```xml
<?xml version="1.0" encoding="UTF-8"?>
<Response>
    <Gather action="iamhuman.xml">
        <Say>Press any key to accept this call</Say>
    </Gather>
    <Hangup/>
</Response>
```

6. Since the person who was called did press a key, we assume he or she is a real person, and not a machine, and connect the call.

```xml
<?xml version="1.0" encoding="UTF-8"?>
<Response>
  <Say>Connecting</Say>
</Response>
```

7. Finally, you have to point your Twilio phone number to it.

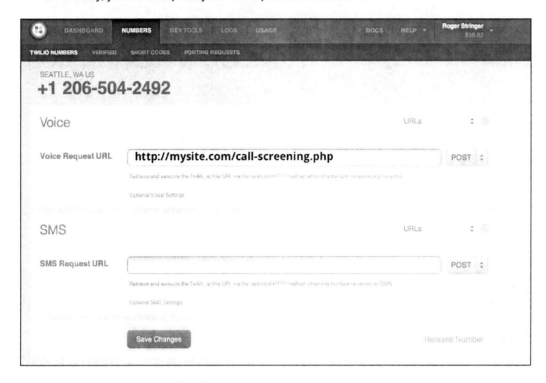

Insert the URL to this page in the **Voice Request URL** box. Then, any calls that you receive at this number will be processed via `call-screening.php`.

How it works...

In steps 1 and 2, we downloaded and installed the Twilio Helper Library for PHP. This library is at the heart of your Twilio-powered apps.

In step 3, we uploaded `config.php` that contains our authentication information to talk to Twilio's API.

In step 4, we uploaded `call-screening.php`; in steps 5 and 6, we created `areyouhuman.xml` and `iamhuman.xml`.

Finally, in step 7, we configured a phone number to direct all calls to `call-screening.php`.

Now, all calls to this phone number are sent directly to `call-screening.php`. The app then directs the call to the first number on the `$numbers` list.

When the call is answered, we trigger `areyouhuman.xml`, which waits for the person who answered the call to hit any key on their phone.

When any key is pressed, we can safely assume that the person who answered the phone is a person and not an answering machine; we then connect them to `iamhuman.xml` that then connects the call. If no key is pressed, we try the next number on the list.

As I mentioned, this type of recipe comes in handy for having multiple on-call agents in departments such as Support and Sales.

Buying a phone number

Buying a phone number is an integral part of the Twilio system. If you have multiple users, you can assign each user their own phone number.

Twilio gives you options to pass on numbers to your users, so you can actually search for phone numbers.

You can search by postal code; patterns, such as STRINGER; or for phone numbers near your location.

I've found this ability handy for systems with multiple users or for setting up business numbers for various purposes, such as sales, support, or unique phone numbers for campaigns that are being run at the time.

Getting ready

The complete source code for this recipe can be found in the `Chapter2/Recipe3` folder.

How to do it...

Are you ready to learn how to buy a phone number? This recipe will take you step by step through the process.

1. Download the Twilio Helper Library from `https://github.com/twilio/twilio-php/zipball/master` and unzip it.

2. Upload the `Services/` folder to your website.

3. Upload `config.php` to your website and make sure the following variables are set:
   ```php
   <?php
     $accountsid = '';  //  YOUR TWILIO ACCOUNT SID
     $authtoken = '';  //     YOUR TWILIO AUTH TOKEN
     $fromNumber = '';  //  PHONE NUMBER CALLS WILL COME FROM
   ?>
   ```

4. Create a file on your website called `buy-phone-number.php`, with the following code:

```php
<?php
  include 'Services/Twilio.php';
  include("config.php");
  $client = new Services_Twilio($accountsid, $authtoken);
?>
  <h3>Find a number to buy</h3>
  <?php if(!empty($_GET['msg'])): ?>
    <p class="msg"><?php echo htmlspecialchars($_GET['msg']); ?></p>
  <?php endif;?>
  <form method="POST" action="search.php">
  <label>near US postal code (e.g. 94117): </label><input type="text" size="4" name="postal_code"/><br/>
  <label>near this other number (e.g. +14156562345): </label><input type="text" size="7" name="near_number"/><br/>
  <label>matching this pattern (e.g. 415***MINE): </label><input type="text" size="7" name="contains"/><br/>
    <input type="hidden" name="action" value="search" />
    <input type="submit" name="submit" value="SEARCH"/>
  </form>
```

5. Create a file on your website called `search.php`, with the following code:

```php
<?php
  include 'Services/Twilio.php';
  include("config.php");
  $client = new Services_Twilio($accountsid, $authtoken);

  $SearchParams = array();
  $SearchParams['InPostalCode'] = !empty($_POST['postal_code']) ? trim($_POST['postal_code']) : '';
  $SearchParams['NearNumber'] = !empty($_POST['near_number']) ? trim($_POST['near_number']) : '';
  $SearchParams['Contains'] = !empty($_POST['contains'])? trim($_POST['contains']) : '' ;
  try {
    $numbers = $client->account->available_phone_numbers->getList('US', 'Local', $SearchParams);
    if(empty($numbers)) {
      $err = urlencode("We didn't find any phone numbers by that search");
      header("Location: buy-phone-number.php?msg=$err");
      exit(0);
    }
  } catch (Exception $e) {
```

```php
      $err = urlencode("Error processing search:
{$e->getMessage()}");
      header("Location: buy-phone-number.php?msg=$err");
      exit(0);
   }
?>
   <h3>Choose a Twilio number to buy</h3>
   <?php foreach($numbers->available_phone_numbers as $number){ ?>
   <form method="POST" action="buy.php">
   <label><?php echo $number->friendly_name ?></label>
   <input type="hidden" name="PhoneNumber" value="<?php echo
$number->phone_number ?>">
   <input type="hidden" name="action" value="buy" />
   <input type="submit" name="submit" value="BUY" />
   </form>
   <?php } ?>
```

6. Create a file on your website called buy.php, with the following code:

```php
<?php
   include 'Services/Twilio.php';
   include("config.php");
   $client = new Services_Twilio($accountsid, $authtoken);

   $PhoneNumber = $_POST['PhoneNumber'];
   try {
      $number = $client->account->incoming_phone_numbers-
>create(array(
         'PhoneNumber' => $PhoneNumber
      ));
   } catch (Exception $e) {
      $err = urlencode("Error purchasing number:
{$e->getMessage()}");
      header("Location: buy-phone-number.php?msg=$err");
      exit(0);
   }
   $msg = urlencode("Thank you for purchasing $PhoneNumber");
   header("Location: buy-phone-number.php?msg=$msg");
   exit(0);
   break;
?>
```

How it works...

In steps 1 and 2, we downloaded and installed the Twilio Helper Library for PHP. This library is at the heart of your Twilio-powered apps.

In step 3, we uploaded `config.php` that contains our authentication information to communicate with Twilio's API.

When a user goes to `buy-phone-number.php`, they are presented with a set of options. He/she can search by the postal code, phone number, or phone patterns.

Once they perform the search, we return a list of phone numbers. The user can then buy any number he/she chooses and that number then belongs to him/her.

Integrate this into your web apps and let your users add their own phone numbers to their accounts.

Setting up a voicemail system

All companies need a voicemail system, from a small one-person company to a big 100-person company.

This voicemail system will be set up as one big mailbox that people can call into and leave a message. The message is then e-mailed to you along with a transcription of the message.

Getting ready

The complete source code for this recipe can be found in the `Chapter2/Recipe4` folder.

How to do it...

Let's build a simple voicemail system that can serve as a mailbox for your company.

1. Download the Twilio Helper Library from `https://github.com/twilio/twilio-php/zipball/master` and unzip it.

2. Upload the `Services/` folder to your website.

3. Upload `config.php` to your website and make sure the following variables are set:

```php
<?php
  $accountsid = '';  //  YOUR TWILIO ACCOUNT SID
  $authtoken = '';  //      YOUR TWILIO AUTH TOKEN
  $fromNumber = '';  //  PHONE NUMBER CALLS WILL COME FROM
?>
```

4. Create a file on your website called `voicemail.php`, with the following code:

```php
<?php
include 'Services/Twilio.php';
include("config.php");

$myemail = 'MYEMAIL@me.com';
$message = 'I am not available right now. Please leave a
message.';
$transcribe = true;

$client = new Services_Twilio($accountsid, $authtoken);
$response = new Services_Twilio_Twiml();

$headers = 'From: voicemail@mywebsite.com' . "\r\n" .'Reply-To:
voicemail@mywebsite.com' . "\r\n" .'X-Mailer: Twilio Voicemail';

$from = strlen($_REQUEST['From']) ? $_REQUEST['From'] : $_
REQUEST['Caller'];
$to = strlen($_REQUEST['To']) ? $_REQUEST['To'] : $_
REQUEST['Called'];

if( strtolower($_REQUEST['TranscriptionStatus']) == "completed") {
  $body = "You have a new voicemail from " . ($from) . "\n\n";
  $body .= "Text of the transcribed voicemail:\n{$_
REQUEST['TranscriptionText']}.\n\n";
  $body .= "Click this link to listen to the message:\n{$_
REQUEST['RecordingUrl']}.mp3";
  mail($myemail, "New Voicemail Message from " . ($from), $body,
$headers);
  die;
} else if(strtolower($_REQUEST['TranscriptionStatus']) ==
"failed") {
  $body = "You have a new voicemail from ".($from)."\n\n";
  $body .= "Click this link to listen to the message:\n{$_
REQUEST['RecordingUrl']}.mp3";
  mail($myemail, "New Voicemail Message from " . ($from), $body,
$headers);
  die;
} else if(strlen($_REQUEST['RecordingUrl'])) {
  $response->say("Thanks.  Good bye.");
  $response->hangup();
  if(strlen($transcribe) && strtolower($transcribe) != 'true') {
    $body = "You have a new voicemail from ".($from)."\n\n";
    $body .= "Click this link to listen to the message:\n{$_
REQUEST['RecordingUrl']}.mp3";
```

```php
        mail($myemail, "New Voicemail Message from " . ($from), $body,
$headers);
    }
} else {
  $response->say( $message );
  if( $transcribe )
    $params = array("transcribe"=>"true",
"transcribeCallback"=>"{$_SERVER['SCRIPT_URI']}");
  else
    $params = array();
  $response->record($params);
}
$response->Respond();
?>
```

> This voicemail system is pretty basic. We repeat a message and then prompt the caller to leave their message; we then supply an e-mail of the link to the recording as well as the transcription, if transcribing was turned on.

5. To have a number point to this script, upload `voicemail.php` somewhere and then point your Twilio phone number to it.

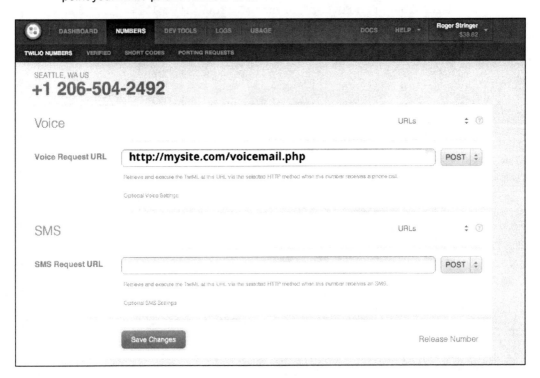

Insert the URL to this page in the **Voice Request URL** box. Then, any calls that you receive at this number will be processed via `voicemail.php`.

How it works...

In steps 1 and 2, we downloaded and installed the Twilio Helper Library for PHP. This library is at the heart of your Twilio-powered apps.

In step 3, we uploaded `config.php` that contains our authentication information to communicate with Twilio's API.

In step 4, we uploaded `voicemail.php`.

Finally, in step 5, we configured a phone number to direct all calls to `voicemail.php`.

When a user calls into this number, we supply a voicemail box and then send you an e-mail containing a transcription of the message, a link to the recording, and the name of the caller.

Building an emergency calling system

I'm a type-2, insulin-dependent diabetic. I also drive two hours every day—to my office and back. So, after I spent a week in the hospital last year, I decided to set up an **In Case Of Emergency** (**ICE**) system so that I could call one number and have it try multiple numbers at once.

Getting ready

The complete source code for this recipe can be found in the `Chapter2/Recipe4` folder.

How to do it...

This emergency calling system will try a group of numbers at the same time; the first number to answer will get connected.

1. Download the Twilio Helper Library from `https://github.com/twilio/twilio-php/zipball/master` and unzip it.

2. Upload the `Services/` folder to your website.

3. Upload `config.php` to your website and make sure the following variables are set:

    ```php
    <?php
      $accountsid = '';  //  YOUR TWILIO ACCOUNT SID
      $authtoken = '';  //      YOUR TWILIO AUTH TOKEN
      $fromNumber = '';  //  PHONE NUMBER CALLS WILL COME FROM
    ?>
    ```

4. Create a file on your website called `ice.php`, with the following code:

```php
<?php
session_start();
include 'Services/Twilio.php';
include("config.php");
$client = new Services_Twilio($accountsid, $authtoken);
$response = new Services_Twilio_Twiml();
$timeout = 20;
$phonenumbers = array(
   '1234567890',
   '1234567891'
);
$dial = $response->dial(NULL, array('callerId' => $fromNumber));
foreach($phonenumbers as $number){
   $dial->number( $number );
}
header ("Content-Type:text/xml");
print $response;
?>
```

5. To have a number point to this script, upload `ice.php` somewhere and then point your Twilio phone number to it.

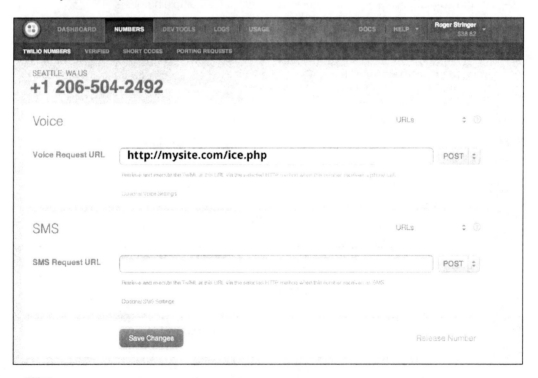

Insert the URL to this page in the **Voice Request URL** box. Then, any calls that you receive at this number will be processed via ice.php.

How it works...

In steps 1 and 2, we downloaded and installed the Twilio Helper Library for PHP. This library is at the heart of your Twilio-powered apps.

In step 3, we uploaded config.php that contains our authentication information to communicate with Twilio's API.

In step 4, we uploaded ice.php.

Finally, in step 5, we configured a phone number to direct all calls to ice.php.

We then set up the $phonenumbers array with the phone numbers in this recipe, which you should try.

When a user calls the phone number you assigned to ice.php, it tries all the numbers in the $phonenumber array at once and connects the call to the first one that answers.

You can store this number at a prominent location on your contacts list so that, in case of emergencies, you can quickly dial the number. I usually save the number to a contact named ICE and add it to favorites so that it is at the top of the list.

3
Conducting Surveys via SMS

In this chapter we will cover the following:

▸ Letting users subscribe to receive surveys

▸ Building a survey tree

▸ Sending a survey to your users

▸ Adding tracking for each user

▸ Listening to user responses

▸ Building a chart of responses

Introduction

One of the common requests I receive from clients is the option to send surveys via SMS. This chapter is based on the survey builders I've built for my clients.

Surveys are handy for seeing what features users want to build into a web app next, running contests, and generally gathering opinions.

In the first section, you'll have a way to let your users subscribe to your surveys. Then you'll build a survey builder that lets you view stats on sent surveys and also send new surveys. We'll include tracking here so that you can see what responses people send back and also give users the ability to unsubscribe from surveys.

Finally, we'll add some handy charting so that we can view the survey results on a nice chart.

This chapter will involve some SQL; you can find the sql file in the Chapter3/ folder.

We're also going to use a class to use PHP's PDO library for database handling. This file is called `pdo.class.php` and can be found in the `Chapter3/` folder.

There are many ways to connect to databases in PHP, but I prefer the PDO driver because you can actually quickly tell it to connect to MySQL, SQLite, or PostgreSQL. In this book, we'll be using MySQL when we use databases.

Why use PDO instead of the standard MySQL functions?

There are several ways to connect to a MySQL database in PHP. You can use `mysql_*` functions that have become deprecated, old, and slow. You can also use `mysqli_*` functions that are slowly replacing `mysql_*` functions; however, they are also slow.

PDO stands for **PHP Data Objects**; it recently replaced the original MySQL library for the purpose of talking to databases. It also has support for PostgreSQL and SQLite.

The PDO extension defines a lightweight, consistent interface for accessing databases in PHP. Each database driver that implements the PDO interface can expose database-specific features as regular extension functions.

PDO is also nice because it provides a data-access abstraction layer, which means that, regardless of the database you use, you employ the same functions to issue queries and fetch data.

The process we use to talk to our MySQL databases is a class called `pdo.class.php`. We use it to talk to our databases using the PDO library.

Our `pdo.class.php` file will contain the following code:

```php
<?php

class Db {
  private $pdoInstance;
  private static $instance;
  private function __construct() {
    global $dbhost,$dbname,$dbuser,$dbpass;
    $this->pdoInstance = new PDO("mysql:host={$dbhost};dbname={$dbname}",$dbuser,$dbpass);
    $this->pdoInstance->setAttribute(PDO::ATTR_ERRMODE, PDO::ERRMODE_EXCEPTION);
    $this->pdoInstance->exec("set names 'utf8'");
  }
  private function __clone() {}
  public static function singleton() {
    if (!isset(self::$instance)) {
```

```
        $c = __CLASS__;
        self::$instance = new $c;
    }
    return self::$instance;
}
/* pdo functions */
public function quote($str){
    return $this->pdoInstance->quote($str);
}
public function lastInsertId(){
    return $this->pdoInstance->lastInsertId();
}
public function query($str){
    try {
        return $this->pdoInstance->query($str);
    } catch (PDOException $e) {
        echo "Error : <br />".$str."<br />". $e->getMessage() . "<br
/>".$e->getTraceAsString();
        exit;
    }
}
public function exec($str){
    try {
        return $this->pdoInstance->exec($str);
    } catch (PDOException $e) {
        echo "Error : <br />".$str."<br />". $e->getMessage() . "<br
/>".$e->getTraceAsString();
        exit;
    }
}

}
```

Our PDO class is a handy database wrapper that we will use for most chapters in this book.

The main functions of our class that you need to know are mentioned below.

To establish a connection, or use an already established connection, use the following code snippet:

```
$pdo = Db::singleton();
```

This call populates the $pdo variable using a singleton. This way, we only have one database connection and, essentially, only one instance of our database class running.

This prevents incidents that may accidentally result in the creation of multiple connections, and also prevents having to pass global variables throughout the site. Instead, we can just call $pdo = Db::singleton(); and we return our PDO class object.

To perform queries, such as select statements, we use the following:

```
$result = $pdo->query("SELECT * from table");
$total = $result->rowCount();
while( $row = $result->fetch() ){
echo $row['name'];
}
```

This query will return a result set based on our query, which is stored in the $result variable.

We can then retrieve a total row count using the $result->rowCount(); function.

We can also set up a while loop to populate the $row variable with a new record on each iteration; that is, the $row = $result->fetch() call.

If we want to perform a query that doesn't actually return any results, we can use the following call:

```
$db->exec("INSERT INTO table SET name='test';");
```

This will let us make a call to our table and insert, update, or delete data without caring about the result returned.

Oh, and one more thing; if you do perform an insert, you may want the last inserted ID, which you can get by calling the following function after you call the $db->exec() function:

```
$pdo->lastInsertId();
```

This only works on inserts, not updates.

You may also notice that, in the class, we wrap all of our queries in a try{}exception{} function, which lets us kill the system in case of errors and display the problem right away.

This has come in handy many times for me during development on projects.

Ok, now let's continue with our chapter.

Letting users subscribe to receive surveys

Before we can send surveys, we want to have a way for users to subscribe to them.

This form will let users enter their phone numbers and add them to the survey system.

You can put this page on a section of your website and allow people to sign up to receive your surveys.

Getting ready

The complete source code for this recipe can be found in the `Chapter3/` folder of the code bundle available at `http://www.packtpub.com/support`.

How to do it...

Let's build a handy system to let users subscribe to receive our surveys. Perform the following steps:

1. Load the `sql.sql` file into your database.

2. Upload `config.php` to your website and make sure the following variables are set:
    ```php
    <?php
    $accountsid = '';  //  YOUR TWILIO ACCOUNT SID
    $authtoken = '';  //  YOUR TWILIO AUTH TOKEN
    $fromNumber = '';  //  PHONE NUMBER CALLS WILL COME FROM

    $dbhost = '';  //  YOUR DATABASE HOST
    $dbname = '';  //  YOUR DATABASE NAME
    $dbuser = '';  //  YOUR DATABASE USER
    $dbpass = '';  //  YOUR DATABASE PASS
    ?>
    ```

3. Upload `pdo.class.php` to your website.

4. Upload a file on your web server called `subscribe.php`, with the following content:
    ```php
    <?php
    include("config.php");
    include("pdo.class.php");
    include 'Services/Twilio.php';

    $action = isset($_GET['action']) ? $_GET['action'] : null;
    switch($action){
      case 'save':
        $fields = array('phone_number','status');
        $pfields = array();
        $_POST['status'] = 1;
        foreach( $fields as $k){
          $v = $_POST[$k];
          $pfields[] = "{$k} = '{$v}'";
        }
        $sql = "INSERT INTO subscribers SET ".implode(",",$pfields);
        $pdo = Db::singleton();
        $pdo->exec($sql);
        $qid = $pdo->lastInsertId();
    ```

```
        if( isset($qid) && !empty($qid) ){
?>
        <p>Thank you, you have been subscribed to receive surveys</
p>
<?php
        }
    default:
?>
        <h2>Subscribe to receive surveys</h2>
        <form method="POST" action="subscribe.php?action=save">
        <table>
        <tr>
          <td>Please enter your phone number</td>
          <td><input type="text" name="phone_number" /></td>
        </tr>
        </table>
        <button type="submit">Save</button>
        </form>
<?php
        break;
}
?>
```

How it works...

In step 1, we set up our database; in step 2, we configured the settings.

In step 4, we uploaded `subscribe.php`. The `subscribe.php` file gives users a form where they enter their phone number and get added to the survey. This can work inside a Sales page on your website, where you want people to subscribe to your surveys.

I prefer letting users subscribe for surveys themselves rather than manually adding users to surveys, as it lets us get a better grasp on the system. When we give a subscriber some sort of incentive to sign up for a survey, they are more likely to reply to the surveys we send them. For example, we could use this as a contest, where each subscriber is entered into a draw for a prize, but only if they reply to our surveys.

Building a survey tree

The survey builder performs three functions: it shows you the stats on sent surveys, lets you send unsent surveys, and lets you build your new surveys.

Surveys in this system are simple: one question and six possible answers.

Each answer will be assigned a number of 1 to 6.

Getting ready

The complete source code for this recipe can be found in the `Chapter3/` folder.

How to do it...

We've got subscribers but we need to send them what they've subscribed to. This recipe will set up our survey builder. We'll also build a home page as part of our builder, where we can choose to send surveys or view results.

1. Download the Twilio Helper Library from `https://github.com/twilio/twilio-php/zipball/master` and unzip the file.

2. Upload the `Services/` folder to your website.

3. Create a file on your website and name it `survey-builder.php`. The file will have the following content:

```php
<?php
include("config.php");
include("pdo.class.php");
include 'Services/Twilio.php';
switch($_GET['action'] ){
  case 'save':
    $fields = array('question','answer1','answer2','answer3','answ
er4','answer5','answer6','status');
    $pfields = array();
    foreach( $fields as $k){
      $v = $_POST[$k];
      $pfields[] = "{$k} = '{$v}'";
    }
    $sql = "INSERT INTO survey SET ".implode(",",$pfields);
    $pdo = Db::singleton();
    $pdo->exec($sql);
    $qid = $pdo->lastInsertId();
    if( isset($qid) && !empty($qid) ){
?>
      <a href="send-survey.php?qid=<?=$qid?>">Send survey</a> or
<a href="survey-builder.php">Return to home</a>
<?php
    }
  case 'build':
    include("buildform.php");
    break;
  default:
    include("home.php");
    break;
}
?>
```

The `survey-builder.php` file is the root of our system as it handles saving surveys and displaying results.

4. Now, upload `buldform.php` (bearing the following content) to your website.

```html
<h2>Prepare your survey</h2>
<form method="POST" action="survey-builder.php?action=save">
<table>
<tr>
  <td>Question</td>
  <td><input type="text" name="question" /></td>
</tr>
<?php
for($i = 1;$i<= 6;$i++){
?>
  <tr>
    <td>Answer <?=$i?></td>
    <td><input type="text" name="answer<?=$i?>" /></td>
  </tr>
<?php
}
?>
</table>
<button type="submit">Save</button>
</form>
```

 `buildform.php` is the form for building surveys.

5. Upload `home.php` (bearing the following content) to your website:

```php
<a href="survey-builder.php?action=build">Add new survey</a><hr />
<h2>Pending Surveys</h2>
<table width=100%>
<?php
$res = $pdo->query("SELECT * FROM survey WHERE status=0");
while( $row = $res->fetch() ){
?>
<tr>
   <td><?=$row['question']?></td>
   <td><a href="send-survey.php?qid=<?=$row['ID']?>">Send</a></td>
</tr>
<?php
}
```

```
?>
</table>
<br />
```

The first part of this file displays surveys that have not been sent yet. The second part displays surveys that have been sent, and a link to view responses.

```
<h2>Sent Surveys</h2>
<table width=100%>
<?php
$res = $pdo->query("SELECT * FROM survey WHERE status=1");
while( $row = $res->fetch() ){
?>
<tr>
  <td><?=$row['question']?></td>
  <td><a href="view-survey.php?qid=<?=$row['ID']?>">View
Responses</a></td>
</tr>
<?php
}
?>
</table>
```

How it works...

In steps 1 and 2, we downloaded and installed the Twilio Helper Library for PHP, which is at the heart of your Twilio-powered apps.

Finally, in steps 3, 4, and 5, we created `survey-builder.php`, `buildform.php`, and `home.php` respectively.

When you first load the survey builder, you will get a list of surveys; you can view the stats or send pending surveys. Once you choose to build a new survey, you will get a form that lets you build the survey with a list of answers.

Once you save the survey, you can choose to send it right away or return to the index page.

On the index of surveys, we display unsent surveys and sent surveys.

Unsent surveys will have a link that you can use to send them, whereas sent surveys will have a link to view the results. We'll cover both of these capabilities in upcoming recipes in this chapter.

Sending a survey to your users

Ok, we've built the survey. Now how do we send it to our subscribers?

When you're ready to send the survey to your subscribers, this recipe will gather all active subscribers together, build the message, and send it.

It will then record the response for tracking so that we can see which answer is the popular choice or not.

Getting ready

The complete source code for this recipe can be found in the Chapter3/ folder.

How to do it...

Ok, let's send our survey to our users. In the same place you uploaded the files in the previous recipe, create a new file and name it send-survey.php:

```php
<?php
include("config.php");
include("pdo.class.php");

include 'Services/Twilio.php';

$qid = $_GET['qid'];

$_SESSION['survey'] = $qid;    // we store the survey in session so we
can retrieve it later

$pdo = Db::singleton();

$client = new Services_Twilio($accountsid, $authtoken);

$survey = $pdo->query("SELECT * FROM survey WHERE ID='{$qid}'");
if( $survey->rowCount() >= 1 ){
  $survey = $survey->fetch();
  $message = array();
  $message[] = $survey['question'];
  for($i = 1;$i<= 6;$i++){
    $k = 'answer'.$i;
```

```
        if( !empty($survey[ $k ]) ){
          $message[] = $i." - ".$survey[ $k ];
        }
      }
    $message[] = "Reply with the number corresponding to your answer";
    $cnt = count( $message );
    $res = $pdo->query("SELECT ID,phone_number FROM subscribers WHERE
status='1'");
    while( $row = $res->fetch() ){
      $ph = $row['phone_number'];
      $i = 1;
      foreach($message as $m){
        $m = $m . "({$i} / {$cnt})";
        $smsg = $client->account->sms_messages->create( $fromNumber,
$ph, $m );
        $sid = $smsg->sid;
        $sql = "INSERT INTO responses SET phone_number='{$ph}',question_
id='{$qid}',sms_sid='{$sid}',answer=''";
        $pdo->exec( $sql );
        $i++;
      }
    }
  }
?>
<h2>Survey sent!</h2>
<p><a href="survey-builder.php">Return to home</a></p>
```

How it works...

We can choose to send a survey from the survey builder we built in the first part of this chapter.

When we send it, it loads this recipe and grabs a list of subscribers. Each subscriber is sent a survey with a list of answers.

When we send the survey, each text message is given a unique session ID that we save in the Responses table alongside the receiver's phone number and the ID of the survey that was sent.

Each answer has a number in front of it; when your subscribers reply, they will send the number back to listener.php. This is then recorded in the database and we can build stats based on it.

Adding tracking for each user

We want to be able to track each user's response to the survey we sent and this is how we will do that.

In the previous recipe, we stored the phone number, survey ID, and the unique session ID for each person we sent the survey to.

Now we want to store each user's response for tracking later.

Getting ready

The complete source code for this recipe can be found in the `Chapter3/` folder.

How to do it...

Let's set up `tracker.php` that listens for responses from our subscribers using the following steps:

1. On your web server, create a file and name it `tracker.php` with the following code:

```php
<?php
include("config.php");
include("pdo.class.php");
$pdo = Db::singleton();
if( isset($_POST['Body']) ){
  $phone = $_POST['From'];
  $phone = str_replace('+','',$phone);
  $action = strtolower($_POST['Body']);
  $sid = $_POST['SmsSid'];
  $sql = "UPDATE responses SET answer='{$action}' WHERE phone_
number='{$phone}' AND sms_sid='{$sid}'";
  $pdo->exec( $sql );
  $msg = "Your answer has been recorded";
  print_sms_reply($msg);
}
function print_sms_reply ($sms_reply){
  echo "<?xml version=\"1.0\" encoding=\"UTF-8\"?>\n";
  echo "<Response>\n<Sms>\n";
  echo $sms_reply;
  echo "</Sms></Response>\n";
}
?>
```

2. Finally, you have to point your Twilio phone number to it.

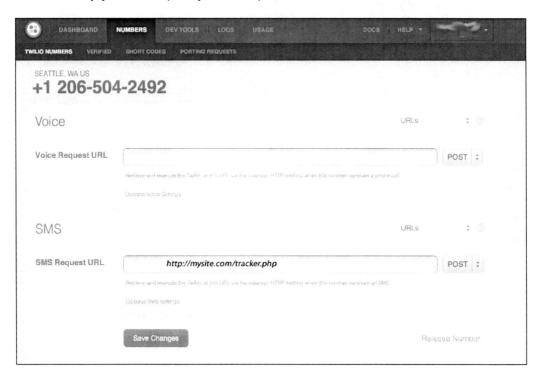

Insert the URL to this page in the **SMS Request URL** box. Then, any calls that you receive on this number will be processed via `tracker.php`.

How it works...

When a user replies to a survey, the `tracker.php` file is triggered.

We then perform a look-up based on their phone number and unique session ID and store their response in the `Responses` table.

Then, when we display the results later, we can use the responses, associate them with the answers we sent, and get a look at what people think.

Listening to user responses and commands

This recipe is the brain of the system; it handles users sending in responses and also handles what to do if a user wants to be unsubscribed. This script will listen on a phone number and do exactly that.

The `listener.php` file replaces `tracker.php`, and it will handle pausing, resuming, and the responses.

Getting ready

The complete source code for this recipe can be found in the `Chapter3/` folder.

How to do it...

Let's build on our previous subscriber tracker and add some extra functionality. We'll call this recipe `listener.php`.

1. Upload the `listener.php` file (with the following content) on your web server.

```php
<?php
include("config.php");
include("pdo.class.php");
$pdo = Db::singleton();
if( isset($_POST['Body']) ){
  $phone = $_POST['From'];
  $phone = str_replace('+','',$phone);
  $action = strtolower($_POST['Body']);
  switch($action){
    case "pause":
      $sql = "UPDATE subscribers SET status=0 WHERE phone_
number='{$phone}'";
      $pdo->exec( $sql );
      $msg = "We have unsubscribed you. Text 'unpause' to be
resubscribed";
      break;
    case "unpause":
      $sql = "UPDATE subscribers SET status=1 WHERE phone_
number='{$phone}'";
      $pdo->exec( $sql );
      $msg = "We have resubscribed you. Text 'pause' to be
unsubscribed";
      break;
    default:
```

```
    $sid = $_POST['SmsSid'];
    $sql = "UPDATE responses SET answer='{$action}' WHERE phone_
number='{$phone}' AND sms_sid='{$sid}'";
    break;
  }
  print_sms_reply($msg);
}
function print_sms_reply ($sms_reply){
  echo "<?xml version=\"1.0\" encoding=\"UTF-8\"?>\n";
  echo "<Response>\n<Sms>\n";
  echo $sms_reply;
  echo "</Sms></Response>\n";
}
?>
```

2. Finally, you have to point your Twilio phone number to it.

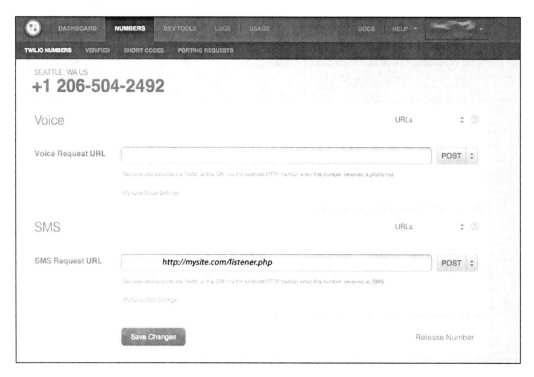

Insert the URL to this page in the **SMS Request URL** box. Then, any calls that you receive on this number will be processed via `listener.php`.

How it works...

The `listener.php` file serves three purposes, all depending on the value of the `$action` variable:

- If `$action` is `"pause"`, the subscriber is unsubscribed and will no longer be sent any surveys

- If `$action` is `"unpause"`, the subscriber is resubscribed and will receive surveys again

- Finally, if `$action` is anything else, it is considered a response and stores the subscriber's answer in the database

Building a chart of responses

We've sent the survey and we've gotten responses; now we want to view results.

We create a chart of the responses we receive from our users; this is assembled onto a page. This handy page will let us see a nice chart of responses to see what people actually think.

We're also going to use the Highcharts PHP library to handle the chart. I like Highcharts because it's easy to customize and fits into any HTML page. The PHP library just helps make it quicker to set up.

Our survey reports will look like the following:

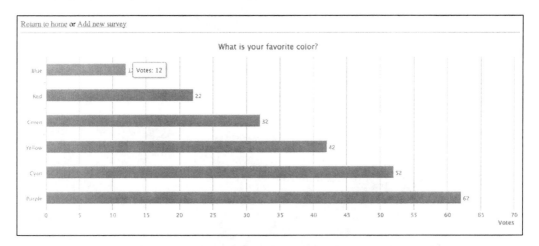

In this example, we've sent a survey that asks our subscribers what their favorite colors are and given them a choice of answers. Each answer is displayed beneath the question, along with the total number of replies for each. As you can see in this example, the color **Purple** was the most popular answer.

The Highcharts library does have other charts in its collection but I like this one because it puts everything right there for all to see.

Getting ready

The complete source code for this recipe can be found in the Chapter3/ folder.

How to do it...

We're sending our surveys and receiving responses. Now let's view the results.

1. Download the Highcharts PHP library from https://github.com/ghunti/ HighchartsPHP.

2. Upload the files to your server in your Services folder.

3. Upload a file on your web server called view-survey.php and containing the following code:

```php
<?php
include("config.php");
include("pdo.class.php");

include("Services/Highchart.php");

$chart = new Highchart();

$qid = $_GET['qid'];

$_SESSION['survey'] = $qid;        // we store the survey in session
// so we can retrieve it later

$pdo = Db::singleton();

$res = $pdo->query("SELECT * FROM survey WHERE ID='{$qid}'");
while( $row = $res->fetch() ){
  $answers = array();
  $ares = $pdo->query("SELECT * FROM responses WHERE question_
id='{$row['id']}' and answer != ''");
  $total = $ares->rowCount();
  while( $ar = $ares->fetch() ){
    $k = $row[ 'answer'.$ar['answer'] ];
    $answers[ $k ]++;
  }
}
```

```php
$qs = array();
$add = array();
foreach($answers as $k=>$c){
  $qs[] = $k;
  $add[] = $c;
}

$chart = new Highchart();
$chart->chart->renderTo = "container";
$chart->chart->type = "bar";
$chart->title->text = $row['question'];
$chart->subtitle->text = "";
$chart->xAxis->categories = $qs;
$chart->xAxis->title->text = null;
$chart->yAxis->min = 0;
$chart->yAxis->title->text = "Votes";
$chart->yAxis->title->align = "high";

$chart->tooltip->formatter = new HighchartJsExpr("function() {
return '' + this.series.name +': '+ this.y;}");

$chart->plotOptions->bar->dataLabels->enabled = 1;
$chart->legend->enabled = false;
$chart->credits->enabled = false;

$chart->series[] = array('name' => "Votes",'data' => $add);
?>
<html>
  <head>
    <title><?=$row['question']?></title>
    <meta http-equiv="Content-Type" content="text/html;
charset=utf-8" />
<?php
    foreach ($chart->getScripts() as $script) {
      echo '<script type="text/javascript" src="' . $script .
'"></script>';
    }
?>
  </head>
  <body>
    <a href="survey-builder.php">Return to home</a> or <a
href="survey-builder.php?action=build">Add new survey</a><hr />
```

```
        <div id="container"></div>
        <script type="text/javascript">
        <?php  echo $chart->render("chart1");  ?>
        </script>
    </body>
</html>
```

How it works...

In steps 1 and 2, we downloaded and installed the Highcharts PHP library.

In step 3, we uploaded view-survey.php.

We've just built one of the most important aspects of our survey tool—a way to graphically show our responses.

We first grab all answers for the question and then we grab all responses. Then we output the data in a nice bar chart.

Using the Highcharts library, we can change this chart to any type we wish pretty quickly. I find the bar chart to be pretty useful, so I'm giving you guys the bar chart to use.

4
Building a Conference Calling System

In this chapter we will cover:

- ▸ Scheduling a conference call
- ▸ Sending an SMS to all participants at the time of the call
- ▸ Starting and recording a conference
- ▸ Joining a conference call from the web browser
- ▸ Monitoring the conference call
- ▸ Muting a participant

Introduction

Conference calling is an important aspect of most businesses. This chapter will help you build a great conference calling app that you can use. It will build a full-fledged conference calling app with multiple conference rooms that people can call.

This chapter will involve some SQL. You can find it in the `sql.sql` file in the `Chapter4/` folder. We're keeping the conference database simple; when we schedule a conference, we enter the names and phone numbers of the participants.

The participants will get a text message with a phone number to call and a room number to enter an hour before the conference begins. This gives everyone time to get situated. We'll also let participants enter a room number and join a conference from their web browsers.

We're also going to build three interesting interfaces: the first lets a person participate in a conference from the web; the second mutes a participant so that they can monitor what's happening but not participate; and the third will give you the ability to mute and unmute callers, which can be handy in cases of seminars.

Scheduling a conference call

The conference call scheduler is going to let you enter details to schedule a conference call. This will let you set up participants, the moderator, and when the call will take place.

Getting ready

The complete source code for this recipe can be found in the `Chapter4/` folder.

How to do it...

Ok, ready? For our first recipe, we're going to build the scheduling and conference management sections.

1. Download the Twilio Helper Library from (`https://github.com/twilio/twilio-php/zipball/master`) and unzip it.

2. Upload the `Services/` folder to your website.

3. Add `sql.sql` to your database.

4. Upload `config.php` to your website and make sure the following variables are set:

    ```php
    <?php
    $accountsid = '';  //  YOUR TWILIO ACCOUNT SID
    $authtoken = '';   //  YOUR TWILIO AUTH TOKEN
    $fromNumber = '';  //  PHONE NUMBER CALLS WILL COME FROM
    $conferenceNumber = '';  //  Number to call into.
    $dbhost = '';  //  YOUR DATABASE HOST
    $dbname = '';  //  YOUR DATABASE NAME
    $dbuser = '';  //  YOUR DATABASE USER
    $dbpass = '';  //  YOUR DATABASE PASS
    ?>
    ```

5. Upload `pdo.class.php` to your website.

6. Create a file on your website called `schedule.php` and add the following code to it:

    ```php
    <?php
    include("config.php");
    include("pdo.class.php");
    include 'Services/Twilio.php';
    ```

```php
include("functions.php");

$action = isset($_GET['action']) ? $_GET['action'] : null;

switch($action){
  case 'save':
        extract($_POST);
        $timestamp = strtotime( $timestamp );
        $sql = "INSERT INTO conference
         SET`name`='{$name}',`timestamp`='{$timestamp}'";
        $pdo = Db::singleton();
        $pdo->exec($sql);
        $qid = $pdo->lastInsertId();
        if( isset($qid) && !empty($qid) ){
             foreach($call_name as $k=>$cname){
                     $cphone = $call_phone[$k];
                     $cstatus = $call_status[$k];
                     $sql = "INSERT INTO callers SET
                      conference_id = '{$qid}',`name` =
                      '{$cname}',`phone_number' =
                      '{$cphone}',status='{$cstatus}'";
                     $pdo->exec($sql);
             }
        }
        break;
  case 'addnew':
        include("form.php");
        break;
  default:
        include("home.php");
        break;
}
```

7. Now let's create a file on your website called `functions.php` and add the following code to it:

```php
<?php
functiongetRecording($caSID){
global $accountsid,$authtoken;
    $version = '2010-04-01';
    $url = "https://api.twilio.com/2010-04-01/Accounts/
            {$accountsid}/Calls/{$caSID}/Recordings.xml";
    $ch = curl_init();
curl_setopt($ch, CURLOPT_URL, $url);
curl_setopt($ch, CURLOPT_RETURNTRANSFER, true);
```

```php
curl_setopt($ch, CURLOPT_USERPWD, "{$accountsid}:{$authtoken}");
curl_setopt($ch, CURLOPT_HTTPAUTH, CURLAUTH_BASIC);
    $output = curl_exec($ch);
    $info = curl_getinfo($ch);
curl_close($ch);
    $output = simplexml_load_string($output);
echo "<table>";
foreach ($output->Recordings->Recording as $recording) {
echo "<tr>";
echo "<td>".$recording->Duration." seconds</td>";
echo "<td>".$recording->DateCreated."</td>";
echo '<td><audio src="https://api.twilio.com/2010-04-01/
Accounts/'.$sid.'/Recordings/'.$recording->Sid.'.mp3" controls
preload="auto" autobuffer></audio></td>';
echo "</tr>";
    }
echo "</table>";
}
?>
```

8. Now, we'll create `home.php`, which will let us display conference calls, and either monitor or review recordings. Add the following code to it:

```php
<ahref="schedule.php?action=addnew">Schedule new conference</a><hr
/>
<h2>Conferences</h2>
<table width=100%>
<?php
  $res = $pdo->query("SELECT * FROM conference ORDER BY
                     `timestamp`");
  while( $row = $res->fetch() ){
        $conference = $client->account->conferences-
           >getIterator(0, 50, array("FriendlyName" =>
           $row['ID']));
?>
        <tr>
          <td><?=$row['name']?></td>
          <td><?=date("m-d-Y ",$row['timestamp'])?></td>
        <td>
<?php  if( $conference->status == "in-progress") { ?>
  <ahref="monitor.php?room=<?=$row['ID']?>">Monitor
  </a> |
  <ahref="view.php?room=<?=$row['ID']?>">View
    Listeners</a>
<?php  }else if( $conference->status == 'completed') {
                getRecording( $conference->sid );
```

```
}else{  ?>
             Not Yet Started
<?php  }      ?>
          </td>
        </tr>
<?php
   }
?>
   </table>
   <br />
```

9. Finally, we'll create `form.php`, which is the actual form used to schedule conference calls. Add the following code to it:

```
<h2>Prepare your conference</h2>
<form method="POST" action="schedule.php?action=save">
<table>
<tr>
   <td>Name</td>
   <td><input type="text" name="name" /></td>
</tr>
<tr>
   <td>Date & Time</td>
   <td>
   <input type="text" name="timestamp"
     placeholder="DD/MM/YY HH:MM"/>
   </td>
</tr>
</table>
<h2>Add Participants</h2>
<table>
<?php
   $limit = 6;
   for($i = 0;$i< $limit;$++){
?>
   <tr>
       <td>Name</td>
       <td><input type="text" name="call_name[]" /></td>
       <td>Phone Number</td>
       <td><input type="text" name="call_phone[]" /></td>
       <td>Moderator?</td>
       <td>
             <select name="call_status[]">
                   <option value="0">No</option>
                   <option value="1">Yes</option>
```

```
                    </select>
            </td>
        </tr>
    <?php
        }
    ?>
    </table>
    <button type="submit">Save</button>
    </form>
```

How it works...

In steps 1 and 2, we downloaded and installed the Twilio Helper Library for PHP; this library is at the heart of your Twilio-powered apps. In step 3, we loaded our database schema into our database.

In step 4, we uploaded `config.php`, which contains our authentication information to talk to Twilio's API. In step 5, we uploaded `pdo.class.php`, which is our class that talks to the database.

Finally, in steps 6 and 7, we created `schedule.php`. This shows you your scheduled conference calls and lets you add new conferences.

In the list of scheduled conference calls, it will check the conference status with Twilio and let you monitor or mute conferences that are in progress or let you view recordings on completed conference calls.

Sending an SMS to all participants at the time of the call

Once it's time to start the conference, you want everyone to know about it. The best way to do that is to send a text message with a number to call to.

This recipe will check once an hour for any upcoming conferences and send a text message to all participants to let them know about it.

Getting ready

The complete source code for this recipe can be found in the `Chapter4/` folder.

How to do it...

This next recipe will create a notification system that will run on an hourly cron job and send an SMS reminder to all participants, and will also have instructions to connect to the conference call.

1. In the same place you uploaded the previous recipe, upload `notify.php` as follows:

```php
<?php
include("config.php");
include("pdo.class.php");
include 'Services/Twilio.php';

$pdo = Db::singleton();
$client = new Services_Twilio($accountsid, $authtoken);

$curtime = strtotime("+1 hour");
$sql = "SELECT * FROM conference where `timestamp` >
$curtime AND notified = 0";

$res = $pdo->query( $sql );
while( $row = $res->fetch() ){
   $msg = "You have a conference call starting in one
   hour. Please call into ".$conferenceNumber." and enter
   ".$row['ID']." as your room";
   $pdo->exec("UPDATE conference SET notified = 1,status=1
   WHERE ID='{$row['ID']}';");
   $sql = "SELECT phone_number FROM callers where
   conference_id='{$row['ID']}'";
   $ares = $pdo->query( $sql );
   while( $arow = $ares->fetch() ){
        $ph = $arow['phone_numer'];
        $client->account->sms_messages->create(
        $fromNumber, $ph, $msg );
   }
}
```

2. Set `notify.php` to run on an hourly cron as follows:

```
0 * * * * /usr/bin/curl -I "http://www.mywebsite.com/notify.php"
```

How it works...

First, we populate the $curtime variable with what the time will be one hour from the present. Then we grab all conferences that are due to start in that time and send a text message to the participants. We also set the conference's status field to 1, which tells the moderator that he/she is allowed to log into it.

Why do we send this one hour earlier instead of exactly when it is scheduled? Excellent question, and one that I've learned to incorporate after plenty of trial and error. If you leave reminders for exactly when you want people to do something, they will most often be late. So, giving them an hour's notice gives everyone a better cushion.

Starting and recording a conference

It's time to start the conference. We've notified everyone about it; now we have to handle what happens when they actually call in.

This conference system has multiple rooms, each with a unique ID. So when people call in, they'll enter a room number, which will add them to that conference room.

Getting ready

The complete source code for this recipe can be found in the Chapter4/ folder.

How to do it...

Ok, this is the big one. This recipe will help us actually start the conference and record the conference as soon as it starts. By recording it, we can go back to it at another time.

We're going to create four files in this recipe.

1. Create a file called start.php and add the following code to it:

```php
<?php
session_start();
include("config.php");
include("pdo.class.php");
include 'Services/Twilio.php';

$pdo = Db::singleton();
$client = new Services_Twilio($accountsid, $authtoken);

if( strlen($_REQUEST['Digits']) ){
    $_SESSION['room'] = $room = $_REQUEST['Digits'];
```

```php
$from = strlen($_REQUEST['From']) ? $_REQUEST['From'] :
$_REQUEST['Caller'];
$to = strlen($_REQUEST['To']) ? $_REQUEST['To'] :
$_REQUEST['Called'];

if(strlen($from) == 11 &&substr($from, 0, 1) == "1") {
    $from = substr($from, 1);
}
$sql = "SELECT * FROM conference where `ID` =
'{$room}'";
$res = $pdo->query( $sql );
$row = $res->fetch();
// is this user a moderator?
$sql = "SELECT * FROM callers where `conference_id` =
'{$room}' AND    `phone_number`='{$from}' AND
status='1' ";
$ares = $pdo->query( $sql );
$arow = $ares->fetch();
if( $arow['phone_number'] == $from ){
    $_SESSION['mod'] = true;
    header("Location: moderator.php");
    die;
}else{
    $_SESSION['mod'] = false;
    header("Location: speaker.php");
    die;
}
}
header('Content-type: text/xml');
echo '<?xml version="1.0" encoding="UTF-8"?>';
?>
<Response>
<Gather numDigits="3" action="start.php">
<Say>Press enter the room number to join your conference</Say>
</Gather>
</Response>
```

2. Now, create a file called `speaker.php` and add the following code to it:

```php
<?php
session_start();
include("config.php");
include("pdo.class.php");
include 'Services/Twilio.php';

$pdo = Db::singleton();
```

```php
$client = new Services_Twilio($accountsid, $authtoken);

$room = $_SESSION['room'];
$sql = "SELECT * FROM conference where `ID` = '{$room}'";
$res = $pdo->query( $sql );
$row = $res->fetch();
header('Content-type: text/xml');
echo '<?xml version="1.0" encoding="UTF-8"?>';
?>
<Response>
<Dial>
<Conference startConferenceOnEnter='false'><?=$row['ID']?></
Conference>
</Dial>
</Response>
```

3. Create a file called `moderator.php` and add the following code to it:

```php
<?php
session_start();
include("config.php");
include("pdo.class.php");
include 'Services/Twilio.php';

$pdo = Db::singleton();
$client = new Services_Twilio($accountsid, $authtoken);

$room = $_SESSION['room'];
$sql = "SELECT * FROM conference where `ID` = '{$room}'";
$res = $pdo->query( $sql );
$row = $res->fetch();
header('Content-type: text/xml');
echo '<?xml version="1.0" encoding="UTF-8"?>';
?>
<Response>
<Dial Record=true>
<Conference
startConferenceOnEnter='true'
endConferenceOnExit='true' muted="false">
<?=$row['ID']?>
</Conference>
</Dial>
</Response>
```

4. Now log in to your Twilio account, go to your phone numbers, select a phone number that people will call, and insert the URL for `start.php` into the box for **Voice** as follows:

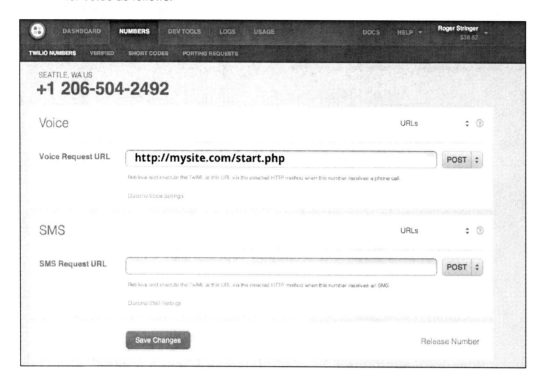

Now, any calls that you receive at this number will be processed via `start.php`.

How it works...

In steps 1, 2, and 3, we created three files: `start.php`, `speaker.php`, and `moderator.php`. In step 4, we set a phone number that handles all incoming calls for the conference system.

When a caller calls the number we entered, Twilio calls `start.php`, which then prompts them to enter a room number; then we check to see if the phone number they are calling from has been set as a moderator's number or not.

If they are a moderator, we call `moderator.php` and start the conference; otherwise, we call `speaker.php` and listen for a moderator to join.

Joining a conference call from the web browser

Some attendees may not want to use their phones for the conference; maybe they want to participate from their computers. This recipe will let them join the same conference via their web browser.

Getting ready

The complete source code for this recipe can be found in the `Chapter4/` folder.

How to do it...

Let's build a browser phone system that will let attendees join a conference call from their web browsers. We will give users the ability to enter a code and join the room of their choice.

1. First, since this is using the Twilio Client, you need to set up a TwiML app under your account.

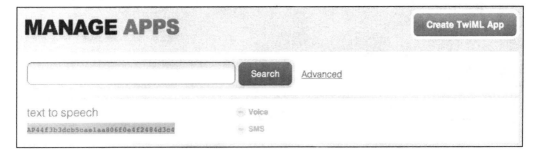

2. Click on the **Create TwiML app** button and enter a name for your app. Also, you'll need to enter a URL for **Voice**. In this case, set it to the URL where you have uploaded `dial-conference.php`; that is, `http://MYWEBSITE.COM/join-conference.php`.

3. Now go back to the application list and you will see your new app. Look at the line directly beneath the name of your app; that is your app's SID. Copy that, as you will need it for this recipe.

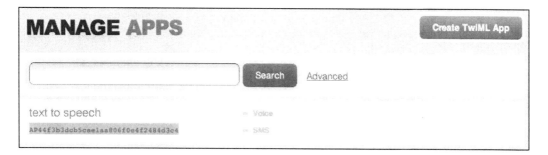

4. Create a file called `join.php` and add the following code to it:

```php
<?php
include("config.php");
include("pdo.class.php");
include 'Services/Twilio.php';
require_once('Services/Twilio/Capability.php');
$pdo = Db::singleton();
$API_VERSION = '2010-04-01';


$APP_SID = 'YOUR APP SID';


$client = new Services_Twilio($accountsid, $authtoken);
include("joinjs.php");
?>
<form method="POST" id="joinform">
  <label>Press enter the room number to join your
   conference</label><br />
  <input type="text" name="room" id="room" />
  <button type="submit">Join</button>
</form>
<div id="choices" style="display:none;">
  <ahref="#" id="linkbtn">Leave</a>
</div>
```

5. Let's create `joinjs.php` as follows:

```php
<?php
$token = new Services_Twilio_Capability($accountsid, $authtoken);
$token->allowClientOutgoing($APP_SID);
?>
<script type="text/javascript" src="https://ajax.googleapis.com/
ajax/libs/jquery/1.6.2/jquery.min.js"></script>
<script type="text/javascript" src="//static.twilio.com/libs/
twiliojs/1.1/twilio.min.js"></script>
<script type="text/javascript">
var conn = null;
$(document).ready(function() {
Twilio.Device.setup("<?php echo $token->generateToken();?>");
  $("#joinform").submit(function(e){
        var name = $("#room").val();
        $("#joinform").hide();
        $("#choices").show();
```

```
joinConference(name, $("#linkbtn") );
        e.preventDefault();
        return false;
    });
      $("li> a").click(function() {
name = $(this).prev().text();
monitorConference(name, $(this));
      });
    });
});
functionjoinConference(name, link) {
if (conn == null){
conn = Twilio.Device.connect( { 'name' : name } );
link.text('Leave');
link.click(function() {
leaveConference(link);
        });
    }
}
functionleaveConference(link) {
conn.disconnect();
conn = null;
  $("#choices").hide();
  $("#joinform").show();
}
</script>
```

6. Now let's create a file called `join-conference.php` and add the following code to it:

```php
<?php
header('Content-type: text/xml');
echo '<?xml version="1.0" encoding="UTF-8"?>';
?>
<Response>
<Dial>
<Conference startConferenceOnEnter='false'><?php echo
htmlspecialchars($_REQUEST['name']); ?>
</Conference>
</Dial>
</Response>
```

How it works...

In steps 1, 2, and 3, we created a new TwiML app that pointed to the `join-conference.php` file. This will tell any applications that use this app's SID what file to call.

In steps 4, 5, and 6, we created `join.php`, which will display all conferences that are currently in progress and let you listen in on any of them. When you join, you are automatically a part of the conference.

Monitoring the conference call

We are also going to add the ability to monitor and listen in on a conference call from the website. This will let us silently listen in on calls.

Monitoring calls can be useful for training purposes; for example, to let someone sit and see how a call works.

Getting ready

The complete source code for this recipe can be found in the `Chapter4/` folder.

How to do it...

Ok, let's build our "big brother" conference monitoring system.

1. First, since this is using the Twilio Client, you need to set up an TwiML app under your account.

2. Click on the **Create TwiML app** button and enter a name for your app. Also, you'll need to enter a URL for **Voice**. In this case, set it to the URL where you have uploaded `dial-conference.php`; that is, `http://MYWEBSITE.COM/dial-conference.php`.

3. Now go back to the application list and you will see your new app. Look at the line directly beneath the name of your app; that is your app's SID. Copy that, as you will need it for this recipe.

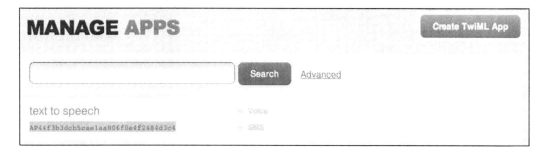

4. Create a file called `monitor.php` and add the following code to it:

```php
<?php
include("config.php");
include("pdo.class.php");
include 'Services/Twilio.php';
require_once('Services/Twilio/Capability.php');
$pdo = Db::singleton();
$API_VERSION = '2010-04-01';

$APP_SID = 'YOUR APP SID';

$client = new Services_Twilio($accountsid, $authtoken);
include("monitorjs.php");
$conferences = $client->account->conferences->getPage(0, 50,
array('Status' => 'in-progress'));
echo '<p>Found '.$conferences->total.' conference(s)</p>';
echo '<ul>';
foreach ($conferences as $conference) {
   echo '<li><span>'.$conference->friendly_name.'</span><a
href="#"">Listen in</a></li>';
}
echo '</ul>';
```

5. Let's create `monitorjs.php` and add the following code to it:

```php
<?php
$token = new Services_Twilio_Capability($accountsid, $authtoken);
$token->allowClientOutgoing($APP_SID);
?>
<script type="text/javascript" src="https://ajax.googleapis.com/
ajax/libs/jquery/1.6.2/jquery.min.js"></script>
<script type="text/javascript" src="//static.twilio.com/libs/
twiliojs/1.1/twilio.min.js"></script>
<script type="text/javascript">
var conn = null;
$(document).ready(function() {
Twilio.Device.setup("<?php echo $token->generateToken();?>");
    $("li> a").click(function() {
    name = $(this).prev().text();
    monitorConference(name, $(this));
    });
});
functionmonitorConference(name, link) {
if (conn == null){
conn = Twilio.Device.connect( { 'name' : name } );
```

```
link.text('Leave');
link.click(function() {
leaveConference(link);
        });
    }
}
functionleaveConference(link) {
conn.disconnect();
conn = null;
link.text('Listen in');
link.click(function() {
name = link.prev().text();
monitorConference(name, link);
    })
}
</script>
```

6. Now, let's create a file called `dial-conference.php` and add the following code to it:

```
<?php
header('Content-type: text/xml');
echo '<?xml version="1.0" encoding="UTF-8"?>';
?>
<Response>
<Dial>
<Conference muted="true" beep="false"><?php echo
htmlspecialchars($_REQUEST['name']); ?></Conference>
</Dial>
</Response>
```

How it works...

In steps 1, 2, and 3, we created a new TwiML app that pointed to the `dial-conference.php` file.

In steps 4, 5, and 6, we created `monitor.php`, which will display all conferences that are currently in progress and let you listen in on any of them. When you join, you are muted, as we want this to be a listener post only.

Muting a participant

Sometimes, when you get a list of conference participants, it's nice to be able to mute someone. Maybe there's too much noise on one end, a participant is being disruptive, or the moderator only wants one speaker to talk (in the case of seminars). This recipe lets you mute and unmute your callers.

Getting ready

The complete source code for this recipe can be found in the Chapter4/ folder.

How to do it...

We're going to create three files in this recipe.

1. The first file is view.php. Add the following code to it:

```php
<?php
include("config.php");
include("pdo.class.php");
include 'Services/Twilio.php';
$pdo = Db::singleton();
$client = new Services_Twilio($accountsid, $authtoken);
?>
<table>
<thead>
<tr>
  <td>Participant</td>
  <td>Muted</td>
  <td></td>
</thead>
<tbody>
<?php
foreach ($client->account->conferences->getIterator(0, 50,
array("Status" => "in-progress","FriendlyName" => $_GET['room']))
as $conference ) {
   foreach ($client->account->conferences->get( $conference->sid
)->participants as $participant) {
?>
         <tr>
           <td>
             <?=$participant->sid?>
           </td>
           <td>
```

```
                    <?=($participant->muted ? "Yes" : "No")?>
                </td>
                <td>
                 <?php  if( $participant->muted ){  ?>
                <ahref="unmute.php?sid=<?=$_GET['room']?>
                  &cid=<?=$participant->sid?>">Unmute</a>
                <?php  }else{  ?>
                <ahref="mute.php?sid=<?=$_GET['room']?>
                  &cid=<?=$participant->sid?>">Mute</a>
                 <?php  }  ?>
                </td>
            </tr>
    <?php
       }
    }
    ?>
    </tbody>
    </table>
```

2. Next, we create `mute.php` and add the following code to it:

```php
<?php
   include("config.php");
   include("pdo.class.php");
   include 'Services/Twilio.php';

   $pdo = Db::singleton();
   $client = new Services_Twilio($accountsid, $authtoken);

   $participant = $client->account->conferences->get(
   $_GET['sid'] )->participants->get( $_GET['cid'] );
   $participant->update(array(
       "Muted" => "True"
   ));
   header("Location:view.php?room=".$_GET['sid']);
   exit;
```

3. And finally we create `unmute.php` and add the following code to it:

```php
<?php
   include("config.php");
   include("pdo.class.php");
   include 'Services/Twilio.php';

   $pdo = Db::singleton();
```

```
$client = new Services_Twilio($accountsid, $authtoken);

$participant = $client->account->conferences->get( $_GET['sid']
              )->participants->get( $_GET['cid'] );
$participant->update(array(
    "Muted" => "False"
));
header("Location:view.php?room=".$_GET['sid']);
exit;
```

How it works...

In step 1, we create `view.php`, which displays a list of participants in a conference room and the option to mute or unmute the caller. In step 2, we created `mute.php`, which is the file that gets called when we choose to mute a caller; once it executes, the caller finds himself muted. In step 3, we created `unmute.php`, which lets us unmute a caller.

It is handy for a moderator to be able to mute or unmute people taking part in a conference. Especially if the conference is a seminar.

5
Combining Twilio with Other APIs

In this chapter, you will learn:

- ▸ Searching for local businesses via text
- ▸ Getting the local weather forecast
- ▸ Searching for local movie listings
- ▸ Searching for classifieds
- ▸ Getting local TV listings
- ▸ Searching Google using SMS
- ▸ Searching the stock market
- ▸ Getting the latest headlines

Introduction

People love to perform local searches. Being able to quickly locate local businesses or local movie listings, find something for sale near them, check the weather, or get TV listings are all local items that people want to look up all the time.

We're also going to let people perform Google searches, grab stock market quotes, and retrieve the latest headlines. We are going to accomplish this using various APIs, such as Yahoo's YQL, Yahoo Weather, Yelp.com, Craigslist, Google, Yahoo Finance, and Yahoo News.

We will use **Application Programming Interface** (**API**); in fact, Twilio itself is an API and we've been using APIs all along. Why use APIs? The answer is pretty simple—you use APIs to gather information from other sources to build apps that are useful to your users.

What is YQL? **Yahoo Query Language** (**YQL**) is an API that lets us talk to other APIs in a method similar to SQL. We'll be using this to get the local weather, find local businesses, and also search for classifieds. You can learn more about YQL at `http://developer.yahoo.com/yql/`.

With YQL, you can send queries such as database queries; for example, to get information on San Francisco, you will write your query like this:

```
select name, country from geo.places where text="san francisco, ca"
```

Then, you'd make your call either via PHP or using JavaScript. You can also test your query directly from the YQL Console at `http://developer.yahoo.com/yql/console/`.

You can see the results of any query by loading it in your browser:

```
http://query.yahooapis.com/v1/public/yql?q=select name, country from
geo.places where text="san francisco, ca"&format=json
```

This URL returns a JSON string based on your query. I've worked with APIs for years on various projects; YQL is the one I return to often, for its sheer power.

We'll also be using other APIs to look up local movies and TV listings. And finally, we'll use Google's API to perform a Google search. We are also going to make this work by simply having someone text with keywords; for example, texting "find pizza" will return pizza restaurants near their current location

How are we going to do this? Simple, Twilio sends us information about where the texter is located when they send us the text message:

```
[Body] => find pizza
[ToZip] => 98101
[FromState] => BC
[ToCity] => SEATTLE
[SmsSid] => SM317729315466f59785223dd04e420728
[ToState] => WA
[To] => +12065042754
[ToCountry] => US
[FromCountry] => CA
[SmsMessageSid] => SM317729315466f59785223dd04e420728
[ApiVersion] => 2010-04-01
[FromCity] => PENTICTON
[SmsStatus] => received
[From] => +12502213321
[FromZip] =>
```

This array tells us the city that the caller is from via the `FromCity` and `FromState` variables. From here, we can perform searches using YQL or other APIs to find local the information. We'll mostly use the `Body`, `FromCountry`, `FromCity`, and `FromState` fields in our search.

Searching for local businesses via text

Ever need to find a local business? You want to know where to find the nearest pizza, sushi, or maybe even a plumber? This script will let you type in `find sushi` on your phone and returns local sushi restaurants. Similarly, typing in `find computers` will find any local computer stores.

We'll use Yahoo's YQL system to perform a local lookup using the Yelp.com API. This way, we're actually using two APIs at one time. YQL lets us perform queries rapidly, so you'll find the speed impressive.

Getting ready

The complete source code for this recipe can be found in the `Chapter5/` folder.

How to do it...

Ok, let's set up our initial app that will let us use Yahoo's YQL service to search for local businesses and restaurants.

1. Download the Twilio Helper Library from (`https://github.com/twilio/twilio-php/zipball/master`) and unzip it.

2. Upload the `Services/` folder to your website.

3. Upload the `config.php` file to your website and make sure the following variables are set:

```php
<?php
$accountsid = '';  //  YOUR TWILIO ACCOUNT SID
$authtoken = '';   //  YOUR TWILIO AUTH TOKEN
$fromNumber = '';  //  PHONE NUMBER CALLS WILL COME FROM
?>
```

4. Create a file called `functions.php` and add the following code to it:

```php
<?php
function remEntities($str) {
  return str_replace("&#8206;","", str_replace(" ","",$str) );
}
function print_sms_reply ($sms_reply){
  echo "<?xml version=\"1.0\" encoding=\"UTF-8\"?>\n";
  echo "<Response>\n";
  if( !is_array($sms_reply) ){
      echo '<Sms>'.$sms_reply.'</Sms>';
  }else{
```

```
            $cnt = count($sms_reply);
            $i = 1;
            foreach($sms_reply as $line){
                    $line = $line." (".$i."/".$cnt.")";
                    echo '<Sms>'.$line.'</Sms>';
                    $i++;
            }
    }
    echo "</Response>\n";
}
function get_query($url){
   $curl = curl_init($url);
   curl_setopt($curl,CURLOPT_HEADER,false);
   curl_setopt($curl,CURLOPT_RETURNTRANSFER,true);
   $data = curl_exec($curl);
   curl_close($curl);
   return $data;
}
function getResultFromYQL($yql_query, $env = '') {
   $yql_base_url =
    "http://query.yahooapis.com/v1/public/yql";
   $yql_query_url = $yql_base_url . "?q=" .
    urlencode($yql_query);
   $yql_query_url .= "&format=json";
   if ($env != '') {
       $yql_query_url .= '&env=' . urlencode($env);
   }
   $session = curl_init($yql_query_url);
   curl_setopt($session, CURLOPT_RETURNTRANSFER, true);
   $json = curl_exec($session);
   curl_close($session);
   return json_decode($json);
}
```

The `functions.php` file is the priority file; it handles various functions related to talking to YQL and responding to texts. Two heavily used functions in this file are `get_query` and `getResultFromYQL`; these are two functions I use quite a lot for talking to APIs.

5. Create a file called `local.php` and add the following code to it:

```
<?php
include('Services/Twilio.php');
include("config.php");
include("functions.php");
if( isset($_POST['Body']) ){
```

```php
$phone = $_POST['From'];
$body = $_POST['Body'];
$from = $_POST['FromCity'].', '.$_POST['FromState'];
$body = strtolower( $body );
$keywords = explode(" ",$body);
$key = $keywords[0];
unset( $keywords[0] );
$keywords = implode(" ",$keywords);
if( file_exists("pages/".$key.".php") ){
// if a file matching this key exists in the pages folder.
For example: movies, weather, find, tv
    include("pages/".$key.".php");
}else{
    $lines = array();
    $lines[] = "Hi, thanks for using local search.
     Please use the following keywords to perform your
     search.";
    $lines[] = "find 'keyword' to search for local
    businesses or restaurants";
    $lines[] = "movies to find local movies";
    $lines[] = "weather to get the local forecast";
    $lines[] = "tv to get the local tv listings and
    see what's on right now";
    $lines[] = "classifieds 'keyword' to search local
    classifieds";
    $lines[] = "search 'keyword' to search Google";
    $lines[] = "stock 'stock symbol' to search the
    stock market";
    $lines[] = "news to return the latest headline
    news";
    print_sms_reply ($lines);
    }
}
exit;
```

6. Create a file called `find.php` in a folder called `pages` and add the following code to it:

```php
<?php
$results = find( $from, $keywords );
$cnt = count( $results->businesses );
$i = 1;
$reply = array();
foreach($results->businesses as $business){
  $business->name = str_replace(" & "," and ",$business->name);
```

```
        $msg = $business->name."\n".$business->address1."\
              n".$business->city ." ".$business->state .",
              ".$business->zip;
        $reply[] = $msg;
        $i++;
}
print_sms_reply( $reply );
function find( $location, $query ){
$yelpql = "use 'http://github.com/spullara/yql-tables/raw/
master/yelp/yelp.review.search.xml' as yelp; select * from
yelp where term='".$query."' and location='".$location."' and
ywsid='AMP_5mIt_VCZiw7xYK0DJw'";
$result = getResultFromYQL( $yelpql );
return $result->query->results;
}
?>
```

7. To have a number point to this script, upload `local.php` somewhere and then point your Twilio phone number to it.

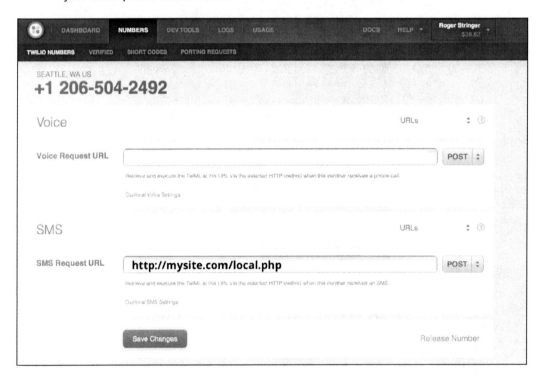

Insert the URL in the box for SMS as shown in the previous screenshot. Any text messages that you receive at this number thereafter will be processed via `local.php`.

How it works...

In steps 1 and 2, we downloaded and installed the Twilio Helper Library for PHP; this library is the heart of your Twilio-powered apps.

In step 3, we loaded our database schema into our database. In step 3, we uploaded `config.php` that contains our authentication information to talk to the Twilio's API.

In steps 4, 5, and 6, we uploaded the `functions.php`, `local.php`, and `find.php` files. And finally, in step 7, we set up our local service on a Twilio phone number. When `local.php` receives a message, it checks the first word. If it is "find," we assume they are looking for a business.

We then use Yahoo's YQL system to query Yelp.com's API and return all businesses that match the keyword searched in the location the person's phone number came from. The query we used to find local businesses is as follows:

```
use 'http://github.com/spullara/yql-tables/raw/master/yelp/yelp.
review.search.xml' as yelp; select * from yelp where term='".$query."'
and location='".$location."' and ywsid='AMP_5mIt_VCZiw7xYK0DJw'";
```

This query tells YQL to use use Yelp.com and search their API for any business in our location that matches the term given; for example, texting in "find sushi" will return a text for each of the four sushi restaurants in my home town.

You may also notice that we used a key called `ywsid`; this is a unique developer key used for Yelp API calls. If you want your own key, you can go to `http://www.yelp.com/developers` and generate one.Then, you can replace the key used by this query with your own.

The `use` command employed by this query is what we used to call an open table. Open tables are XML files that people can write to define their own YQL queries. If you open `http://yqlblog.net/samples/helloworld.xml` in a browser, it will show you an XML file as follows:

```
<?xml version="1.0" encoding="UTF-8"?>
<table xmlns="http://query.yahooapis.com/v1/schema/table.xsd">
  <meta>
    <sampleQuery>select * from {table} where a='cat' and b='dog';
    </sampleQuery>
  </meta>
  <bindings>
    <select itemPath="" produces="XML">
      <urls>
        <url>http://fake.url/{a}</url>
      </urls>
      <inputs>
```

```
            <key id='a' type='xs:string' paramType='path'
             required="true" />
            <key id='b' type='xs:string' paramType='variable'
                required="true" />
        </inputs>
        <execute><![CDATA[
        // Your javascript goes here. We will run it on our servers
            response.object = <item>
                        <url>{request.url}</url>
                        <a>{a}</a>
                        <b>{b}</b>
                    </item>;
        ]]></execute>
      </select>
    </bindings>
  </table>
```

This open table creates a table called `helloworld` and defines which keys you pass to it. So, in this example, we've set up two keys, `a` and `b`, and we've set them both as required. When this is called, it is seen as follows:

```
use "http://yqlblog.net/samples/helloworld.xml";select * from
helloworld where a="cat" and b="dog";
```

We return three fields inside the item record as follows:

```
<item>
  <url>http://fake.url/cat</url>
  <a>cat</a>
  <b>dog</b>
</item>
```

Notice what I mentioned above? We passed the `a` key as `cat` and the `b` key as `dog`, and the query returned the item with a URL containing the value of the `a` key and then the value of `a` and `b` as separate records.

Getting the local weather forecast

The weather lookup portion of this app will work in a similar way to the find portion. When we send a text saying "weather", it returns today's and tomorrow's forecast. We're going to use Yahoo's own weather lookup API for this is already built into Yahoo's YQL system.

We're also going to make use of Yahoo's geo places system that will take our phone number's registered location and return a unique ID that the weather service will use to perform the lookup.

Our query will actually return two messages. The first message is the current forecast; the second message is the forecast for tomorrow.

Getting ready

The complete source code for this recipe can be found in the Chapter5/ folder.

How to do it...

Now, this recipe will extend our search system to include a local weather lookup. Create a file called weather.php in the pages folder and add the following code to it:

```php
<?php
$location = whereami( $from );
$results = weather( $location->woeid );
$forecast = $results->channel->item->forecast;
$today = $forecast[0];
$tomorrow = $forecast[1];
$reply = array();
$reply[] = "Current Conditions: ".$today->text."\nHigh: ".$today-
>high.", Low: ".$today->low;
$reply[] = "Tomorrow: ".$tomorrow->text."\nHigh: ".$tomorrow->high.",
Low: ".$tomorrow->low;
print_sms_reply( $reply );

function whereami($location){
$yql = 'select * from geo.places where text="'.$location.'"';
  $result = getResultFromYQL( $yql );
  return $result->query->results->place;
}
function weather($woeid){
  $yql = 'select * from weather.forecast where woeid='.$woeid;
  $result = getResultFromYQL( $yql );
  return $result->query->results;
}
?>
```

How it works...

In the preceding section, we uploaded weather.php to our pages folder. The weather.php file takes the address from the text and makes a call to yahoo's geo places service to retrieve their WOEID, their unique weather identifier that every city has.

It then makes another YQL call to yahoo weather to return the local weather based on WOEID and sends an SMS reply that contains today's forecast and tomorrow's forecast. These two API calls combine to make a pretty handy weather lookup service.

Searching for local movie listings

For local movie listings, we're moving away from YQL and using Google's movie listing service. You just text "movies" and it will return local movie listings, what time they are playing, and the theatre where it is being screened.

There isn't actually a good API system for looking up movies, so this is kind of a hybrid lookup system that will actually read the content of a web page and return the movie listings.

Scraping, which is what we call this type of lookup, has ups and downs. The upside is that it lets us grab information from web sites that we normally wouldn't be able to get by any other way; however, the downside is that, if the web site changes in any way, the lookup can be broken.

Getting ready

The complete source code for this recipe can be found in the `Chapter5/` folder.

How to do it...

Who wants to go to the movies? This recipe will extend our local search system even further with a handy movie listing.

1. Download the Simple HTML Dom library from `http://simplehtmldom.sourceforge.net/` and upload `simple_html_dom.php` to your web server.

2. Create a file called `movies.php` in the `pages` folder and add the following code to it:

```php
<?php
$movies = movies( $from );
print_sms_reply( $movies );
function movies( $location ){
    require_once('simple_html_dom.php');
    $str = get_query( 'http://www.google.com/movies?near='
        .urlencode($location) );
    $html = str_get_html($str);
    $lines = array();
    foreach($html->find('#movie_results .theater') as $div) {
        $i = 0;
        foreach($div->find('.movie') as $movie) {
        $times = remEntities( strip_tags( $movie-
          >find('.times',0)->innertext ) );
```

```
        $line = strip_tags( $movie->find('.name a',0)-
        >innertext).' [ '.$times.' ] @ '.strip_tags(
        $div->find('h2 a',0)->innertext );
        $lines[ $line ] = $line;
        $i++;
            if( $i == 10)  break;
    }
        break;
    }
    $html->clear();
    return $lines;
}
?>
```

How it works...

The `Movies.php` file is nice. We take the address for the current location and it returns a list of movies. We then use the `simple_html_dom` library to parse the HTML from the returned data and display the movie name, movie time, and also what theatre it is playing at.

This method is another way to get information but it's not as handy as APIs as it can break if someone changes the actual layout of the page we are reading.

Searching for classifieds

For the classifieds search, we're going back to Yahoo's YQL service and we'll be searching using Craigslist. Once set up, you'll be able to type "classifieds ipad" into your phone and it will return any local iPads that are for sale.

Getting ready...

The complete source code for this recipe can be found in the `Chapter5/` folder.

How to do it...

This recipe is mostly for my wife but it's always handy to have a way to search local classifieds sites for items you want to buy. Upload a file called `classifieds.php` to your web server in the pages folder and add the following code to it:

```php
<?php
$results = classifieds( $_POST['FromCity'], $keywords );
$cnt = count( $results->item );
$i = 1;
$reply = array();
```

```
foreach($results->item as $item){
    $item->title = $item->title[0];
    $item->title = str_replace(" & "," and ",$item->title);
    $msg = $item->title."\n".$item->link;
    $reply[] = $msg;
    $i++;
    if( $i == 10)      break;
}
print_sms_reply( $reply );

function classifieds( $location, $query ){
    $yelpql = "USE 'https://raw.github.com/yql/yql-
    tables/master/craigslist/craigslist.search.xml' as
    craiglist.search;select * from craiglist.search where
    location='".$location."' and type="sss" and
    query='".$query."'";
    $result = getResultFromYQL( $yelpql );
    return $result->query->results;
}
?>
```

How it works...

This script works by taking the city you are in and searching craigslist for any matches. It then returns the name of the item as well as a link to it.

This YQL query uses another open table that's already available and performs a lookup based on location, any type, and keyword.

Getting local TV listings

Want to know what's on TV tonight? This query will let you find out what's on for the next 60 minutes. We're going to use the API from Rovi Corp for this. You can get an API key at `http://developer.rovicorp.com/Get_Started`. This isn't as much a local listing as what's on the main TV channels right now.

Getting ready

The complete source code for this recipe can be found in the `Chapter5/` folder.

How to do it...

Let's see what's on TV right now. This recipe will extend our system to let us find out.

1. Get your Rovi Corp API Key from `http://developer.rovicorp.com/Get_Started`.

2. Upload `tv.php` to your `pages` folder and add the following code to it:

```php
<?php
$key = 'Your API Key';
$zip = $_POST['FromZip'];
$cc = $_POST['FromCountry'];

//Get the first TV service for this region:

$url = 'http://api.rovicorp.com/TVlistings/v9/listings/services/
postalcode/'.$zip.'/info?locale=en-US&countrycode='.$cc.'&apikey='
.$key.'&sig=sig';
$services = get_query( $url );
$services = json_decode( $services );
$services = $services->ServicesResult->Services->Service;
if( count($services) ){
  $sid = $services[0]->ServiceId;
  if( !empty($sid) ){
      $url= 'http://api.rovicorp.com/TVlistings/v9/listings/
linearschedule/'.$sid.'/info?locale=en-US&duration=60&inprogress=t
rue&apikey='.$key.'&sig=sig';
      $whatson = get_query( $url );
      $whatson = json_decode( $whatson );
#   echo '<pre>'.print_r($whatson,true).'</pre>';
      $whatson = $whatson->LinearScheduleResult-
      >Schedule->Airings;
      $shows = array();
      $shows[] = "TV Shows starting in the next 60
      minutes are:";
      $i = 0;
      foreach( $whatson as $show ){
      $shows[] = $show->Channel.' - '.$show->Title;
          $i++;
          if( $i == 10)     break;
      }
      print_sms_reply( $shows );
  }
}else{
  print_sms_reply( 'No shows were found for your region.' );
}
```

How it works...

This API lookup uses the Rovi Corp API to find out what's playing locally within the next 60 minutes on TV. You text "tv" and the system returns local TV listings. This makes it handy to see what you want to watch on TV.

Searching Google using SMS

Want to just search the Web for something? This last recipe will let you do just that. This recipe will let us use the "search" keyword to trigger a search in Google and return the top three search results.

To do this, we're going to build a Custom Search Engine and also use Google's API.

Getting ready

The complete source code for this recipe can be found in the `Chapter5/` folder.

How to do it...

And now, the big one. We will now add Google search to our local search system.

1. Get your Google API key from `https://code.google.com/apis/console`.

2. Go to `http://www.google.com/cse/` and create a Custom Search Engine. We want it to search the entire Internet, so make sure you do the following:

   ❑ In the **Sites to Search** field, feel free to enter any domain; we will delete it later

   ❑ Head to the **Setup** tab under **Edit search engine**. In the **Sites to Search** drop-down list, select **Search the entire web but emphasize included sites**

   ❑ Select the domain name that you entered on the list and delete it

   Now you have a Custom Search Engine that searches the entire web. Be sure to copy the CX parameter from your URL; we will be using this later

3. Download the Google API Client for PHP from `https://code.google.com/p/google-api-php-client/`.

4. Unzip the folder and upload it to your web server.

5. Upload `search.php` to your `pages` folder and add the following code to it:

```php
<?php
require_once 'google-api-php-client/src/Google_Client.php';
require_once 'google-api-php-client/src/contrib/Google_
CustomsearchService.php';
session_start();
$client = new Google_Client();
$client->setApplicationName('My Google SMS Search tool');
$client->setDeveloperKey('Your Developer Key Here');
$search = new Google_CustomsearchService($client);
$result = $search->cse->listCse($keywords, array(
  'cx' => 'YOUR CUSTOM SEARCH ENGINE CX HERE',
  'num'=> '3',
));
if( count($results['items']) ){
  $msg = array();
  foreach($results['items'] as $item){
        $msg[] = $item['title']." ".$item['link']);
  }
  print_sms_reply( $msg );
}else{
  print_sms_reply("No matches found");
}
```

Replace `Your Developer Key Here` with the developer key you got from the Google API console, and replace `YOUR CUSTOM SEARCH ENGINE CX HERE` with the CX code we told you to copy in step 2.

How it works

In step 1, we set up our Google API key. In step 2, we created our own Custom Search Engine.

In step 3, we downloaded the Google API key for PHP; in step 4, we uploaded the folder to our web server. Step 5 saw us create our `search.php` file in our pages folder, which lets us perform Google searches from our phones via SMS.

This API look up uses the Google Custom Search Engine API to search the Internet for you. When you text "search" and a keyword, it will return the top three search results for that keyword.

We're using Google's API Client for PHP to do the hard work for this search because it's already set up for us. It's quick and works well.

Searching the stock market

Want to get the latest stock quotes for your favorite stock symbol? This recipe will let us use the "stock" keyword to trigger a lookup of the latest stock quotes.

So for example, sending a text of "stock AAPL" will return the latest stock information for the AAPL symbol.

Getting ready

The complete source code for this recipe can be found in the `Chapter5/` folder.

How to do it...

This recipe will let us search Yahoo Finance for today's price quote by using the stock symbol. Create a file called `stock.php` in the `pages` folder and add the following code to it:

```php
<?php
  $results = stock( $keywords );
  $i = 1;
  $reply = array();
  $quote = $results->quote;
  $msg = $quote->symbol.' - '.$quote->LastTradePriceOnly.' -
   '.$quote->Change.' - '.$quote->PercentChange;
    $reply[] = $msg;
    print_sms_reply( $reply );

function stock( $symbol ){
    $yelpql = "
    USE 'http://www.datatables.org/yahoo/finance/yahoo.finance.quotes.
xml' AS yahoo.finance.quotes;select * from yahoo.finance.quotes where
symbol in ('{$symbol}')";
    $result = getResultFromYQL( $yelpql );
    return $result->query->results;
}
?>
```

How it works...

In step 1, we created our `stock.php` file in our pages folder, which lets us perform the stock quote looks via SMS. This API lookup uses the Yahoo Finance Quote tool in YQL to return today's stock information for the symbol we sent.

When you text "stock" and a stock symbol, you will return today's stock information. Sending "stock AAPL" will return the following format:

```
AAPL - 440.51 - +21.52 - +5.14%
```

The preceding line is the stock symbol, last trade price, price change, and percentage change

Getting the latest headlines

Want to get the latest headlines? This recipe will let us use the "news" keyword to return the ten latest headlines.

Getting ready

The complete source code for this recipe can be found in the Chapter5/ folder.

How to do it...

This recipe will let us search News:used, for the latest headlines from Yahoo News. Create a file called news.php in the pages folder and add the following code to it:

```php
<?php
  $results = news( );
  $i = 1;
  $reply = array();
  foreach($results->item as $item){
        $msg = $item->title;
        $reply[] = $msg;
  }
  print_sms_reply( $reply );

  function news( ){
        $yelpql = 'select title from rss where
        url="http://rss.news.yahoo.com/rss/topstories" LIMIT 10';
        $result = getResultFromYQL( $yelpql );
        return $result->query->results;
  }
?>
```

How it works...

In step 1, we created our news.php file in our pages folder, which lets us return the latest headlines. This API look up uses the Yahoo News RSS feed via YQL to return the ten most recent headlines. This can be handy for being up-to-date or if you just need a conversation starter.

6

Sending and Receiving SMS Messages

In this chapter you will learn:

- ▶ Sending a message from a website
- ▶ Replying to a message from the phone
- ▶ Forwarding an SMS message to another phone number
- ▶ Sending bulk SMS messages to a list of contacts
- ▶ Tracking orders with SMS
- ▶ Sending group chats
- ▶ Sending SMS messages in phone calls
- ▶ Monitoring a website

Introduction

Being able to send SMS messages is a major part of any project that involves phone work. I use it to send reminders, hold chats, and a variety of other tasks related to the projects being used.

In this chapter, we'll send messages from a website, track the received messages, send bulk messages, track orders, host a group chat, and send SMS messages when we receive a phone call.

We're also going to build a simple website monitor that will check a group of websites every five minutes and send you a text if the site is down. By the end of this chapter, there won't be much that you won't be able to do with SMS and it will make for a fun experience to enhance your web apps.

Sending a message from a website

Sending messages from a website has many uses; sending notifications to users is one good example. In this example, we're going to present you with a form where you can enter a phone number and message and send it to your user. This can be quickly adapted for other uses.

Getting ready

The complete source code for this recipe can be found in the `Chapter6/Recipe1/` folder.

How to do it...

Ok, let's learn how to send an SMS message from a website. The user will be prompted to fill out a form that will send the SMS message to the phone number entered in the form.

1. Download the Twilio Helper Library from `https://github.com/twilio/twilio-php/zipball/master` and unzip it.

2. Upload the `Services/` folder to your website.

3. Upload `config.php` to your website and make sure the following variables are set:

```php
<?php
$accountsid = '';  //  YOUR TWILIO ACCOUNT SID
$authtoken = '';   //  YOUR TWILIO AUTH TOKEN
$fromNumber = '';  //  PHONE NUMBER CALLS WILL COME FROM
?>
```

4. Upload a file called `sms.php` and add the following code to it:

```php
<!DOCTYPE html>
<html>
<head>
<title>Recipe 1 - Chapter 6</title>
</head>
<body>
<?php
include('Services/Twilio.php');
include("config.php");
include("functions.php");
$client = new Services_Twilio($accountsid, $authtoken);

if( isset($_POST['number']) && isset($_POST['message']) ){
  $sid = send_sms($_POST['number'],$_POST['message']);
  echo "Message sent to {$_POST['number']}";
```

```
    }
    ?>
    <form method="post">
    <input type="text" name="number" placeholder="Phone Number...."
    /><br />
    <input type="text" name="message" placeholder="Message...." /><br
    />
    <button type="submit">Send Message</button>
    </form>
    </body>
    </html>
```

5. Create a file called functions.php and add the following code to it:

```php
<?php

function send_sms($number,$message){
    global $client,$fromNumber;
    $sms = $client->account->sms_messages->create(
        $fromNumber,
        $number,
        $message
    );
    return $sms->sid;
}
```

How it works...

In steps 1 and 2, we downloaded and installed the Twilio Helper Library for PHP. This library is the heart of your Twilio-powered apps. In step 3, we uploaded config.php that contains our authentication information to talk to Twilio's API.

In steps 4 and 5, we created sms.php and functions.php, which will send a message to the phone number we enter. The send_sms function is handy for initiating SMS conversations; we'll be building on this function heavily in the rest of the chapter.

Replying to a message from the phone

When a user replies to a message from his/her phone, we want to store it in the database so that we can review the messages later.

Getting ready

The complete source code for this recipe can be found in the Chapter6/Recipe2/ folder.

How to do it...

We're going to build a simple app that will receive SMS messages and store them in a database. When we receive SMS messages, we will store them inside the database along with the phone number the message came from and the unique SID.

1. Download the Twilio Helper Library from `https://github.com/twilio/twilio-php/zipball/master` and unzip it.

2. Upload the `Services/` folder to your website.

3. Create a MySQL database and load the contents of `sql.sql` into the database.

4. Upload `config.php` to your website and make sure the following variables are set as follows:

```php
<?php
$accountsid = '';  //  YOUR TWILIO ACCOUNT SID
$authtoken = '';   //  YOUR TWILIO AUTH TOKEN
$fromNumber = '';  //  PHONE NUMBER CALLS WILL COME FROM
$dbhost = '';  //  YOUR DATABASE HOST
$dbname = '';  //  YOUR DATABASE NAME
$dbuser = '';  //  YOUR DATABASE USER
$dbpass = '';  //  YOUR DATABASE PASS
?>
```

5. Upload `listener.php` to your server using the following code:

```php
<?php
   include("config.php");
   include("pdo.class.php");
   include("functions.php");

   $pdo = Db::singleton();

   if( isset($_POST['Body']) ){
        $phone = $_POST['From'];
        $phone = str_replace('+','',$phone);
        $message = $_POST['Body'];
        $sid = $_POST['SmsSid'];
        $now = time();
        $sql = "INSERT INTO messages SET
        `message`='{$message}', `phone_number`='{$phone}',
        `sms_sid`='{$sid}',`date`='{$now}'";
        $pdo->exec( $sql );
        $msg = "Your message has been recorded";
        print_sms_reply($msg);
   }
?>
```

6. Create a file called `functions.php` and add the following code to it:

```php
<?php
function send_sms($number,$message){
  global $client,$fromNumber;
  $sms = $client->account->sms_messages->create(
          $fromNumber,
          $number,
          $message
  );
  return $sms->sid;
}

function print_sms_reply ($sms_reply){
  echo "<?xml version=\"1.0\" encoding=\"UTF-8\"?>\n";
  echo "<Response>\n<Sms>\n";
  echo $sms_reply;
  echo "</Sms></Response>\n";
}
```

7. Finally, you have to direct your Twilio phone number to it:

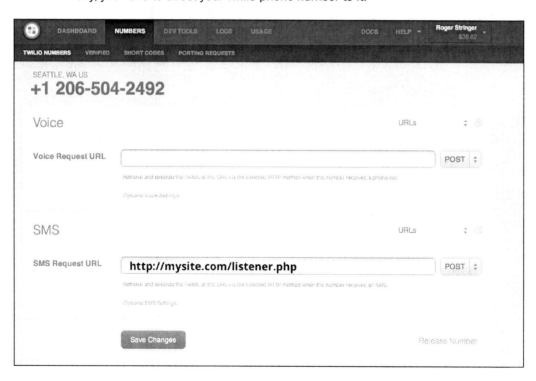

Insert a URL that directs to this page in the **SMS Request URL** box. Then, any calls that you receive at this number will be processed via `listener.php`.

How it works...

In steps 1 and 2, we downloaded and installed the Twilio Helper Library for PHP, which is the heart of your Twilio-powered apps. This library will be used for all communication between your web app and Twilio.

In step 3, we loaded our database schema into our database. In step 4, we uploaded `config.php` that contains our authentication information to talk to Twilio's API.

In step 5, we uploaded `listener.php` to our website, which records all incoming texts. In step 6, we uploaded `functions.php`, which handles the functions required to send and receive messages.

In step 7, we told our Twilio number to direct all SMS messages to `listener.php`. Whenever this number receives a text, it gets stored in the messages table of our database along with the phone number it came from and the SMS session ID. We can use this session ID to piece together a conversation.

Forwarding SMS messages to another phone number

This recipe can be handy when you want to forward SMS messages you received from one phone number on your cell phone.

Getting ready

The complete source code for this recipe can be found in the `Chapter6/Recipe3/` folder.

How to do it...

We're about to build a web app that will listen to incoming SMS messages and forward them to another phone number.

1. Download the Twilio Helper Library from `https://github.com/twilio/twilio-php/zipball/master` and unzip it.
2. Upload the `Services/` folder to your website.
3. Upload `config.php` to your website and make sure the following variables are set:
   ```php
   <?php
   $accountsid = '';   //   YOUR TWILIO ACCOUNT SID
   $authtoken = '';    //   YOUR TWILIO AUTH TOKEN
   $fromNumber = '';   //   PHONE NUMBER CALLS WILL COME FROM
   $toNumber = '';     //   YOUR PHONE NUMBER TO FORWARD SMS TO
   ?>
   ```

4. Upload `forward.php` to your server and add the following code to it:

```php
<?php
  include 'Services/Twilio.php';

  include("config.php");
  include("functions.php");

  $client = new Services_Twilio($accountsid, $authtoken);

  if( isset($_POST['Body']) ){
      header('Content-Type: text/html');
      $from = $_POST['From'];
      $body = $_POST['Body'];
      $msg = '['.$from.'] ' . $body;
      $msg = substr($msg, 0, 160);
      send_sms($toNumber,$msg);
      print_sms_reply( $canned );
  }
```

5. Create a file called `functions.php` and add the following code to it:

```php
<?php
function send_sms($number,$message){
  global $client,$fromNumber;
  $sms = $client->account->sms_messages->create(
        $fromNumber,
        $number,
        $message
  );
  return $sms->sid;
}

function print_sms_reply ($sms_reply){
  echo "<?xml version=\"1.0\" encoding=\"UTF-8\"?>\n";
  echo "<Response>\n<Sms>\n";
  echo $sms_reply;
  echo "</Sms></Response>\n";
}
```

6. Finally, you have to point your Twilio phone number to it:

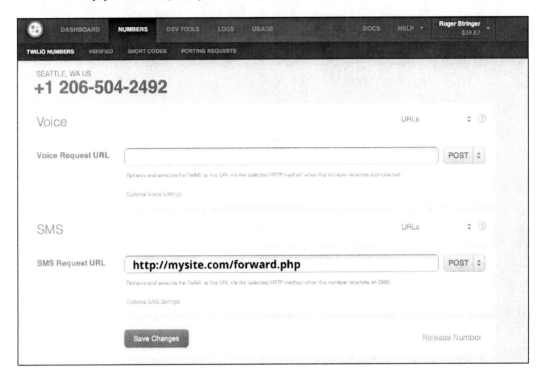

Insert the URL that directs to this page in the **SMS Request URL** box . Then, any calls that you receive at this number will be processed via `forward.php`.

How it works...

In steps 1 and 2, we downloaded and installed the Twilio Helper Library for PHP, which is the heart of your Twilio-powered apps. This library will be used for all communication between your web app and Twilio.

In step 3, we uploaded `config.php` that contains our authentication information to talk to Twilio's API. In step 4, we uploaded `forward.php` to our website, which takes the incoming SMS and forwards it to the phone number we saved in the `$toNumber` variable. It also sends canned messages to the sender using the `$canned` variable from the `config.php` file.

In step 5, we uploaded `functions.php` that handles the functions to send and receive messages. In step 6, we told our Twilio number to direct all SMS messages to `forward.php`.

Now, whenever we receive an SMS message at the number selected, we forward that message to our main phone number and also send a canned response to the sender thanking them for the message.

Sending bulk SMS to a list of contacts

When you have a big product launch and you want to notify your users or send out a promotion, this is the script you would use.

Getting ready

The complete source code for this recipe can be found in the `Chapter6/Recipe4/` folder.

How to do it...

We're going to build an app in this section that will let us send a message to a list of contacts. This is handy for advertising new promotions with your business.

1. Download the Twilio Helper Library from `https://github.com/twilio/twilio-php/zipball/master` and unzip it.

2. Upload the `Services/` folder to your website.

3. Upload `config.php` to your website and make sure the following variables are set:

```php
<?php
$accountsid = '';    //   YOUR TWILIO ACCOUNT SID
$authtoken = '';     //   YOUR TWILIO AUTH TOKEN
$fromNumber = '';    //   PHONE NUMBER CALLS WILL COME FROM
?>
```

4. Upload `bulk.php` to your server and add the following code to it:

```php
<?php
include('Services/Twilio.php');
include("config.php");
include("functions.php");
$client = new Services_Twilio($accountsid, $authtoken);

$people = array(
  "+14158675309" => "Curious George",
  "+14158675310" => "Boots",
  "+14158675311" => "Virgil",
);

$message = "{{name}} Try our new hot and ready pizza!";

foreach ($people as $number => $name) {
  $message = str_replace("{{name}}",$name,$message);
  $sid = send_sms($number, $message);
}
```

5. Upload `functions.php` to your server and add the following code to it:

```php
<?php

function send_sms($number,$message){
  global $client,$fromNumber;
  $sms = $client->account->sms_messages->create(
        $fromNumber,
        $number,
        $message
  );
  return $sms->sid;
}
```

How it works...

In steps 1 and 2, we downloaded and installed the Twilio Helper Library for PHP. This library is the heart of your Twilio-powered apps. In step 3, we uploaded `config.php` that contains our authentication information to talk to Twilio's API.

In step 4, we uploaded `bulk.php`, which handles the actual sending. In step 5, we created `functions.php`, which contains the function that sends our message.

In `bulk.php`, we have an array for `$people`, which stores their phone numbers and names, and we also have the `$message` variable. In this variable, we pass a tag called `{{name}}`. This tag lets us replace the `{{name}}` tag with the person's name as it goes through the list. This is handy for making messages more personal.

Tracking orders with SMS

We've touched on a basic order-tracking recipe in *Chapter 1, Into the Frying Pan*, but this one is going to be a more advanced system. Order tracking is extremely important for any sort of commerce, whether it be e-commerce, call-in orders, or anything that needs a good way to give your customers a way to quickly check their orders.

Making things easy for customers keeps them coming back; having a way for your customers to just text you an order ID and track their purchase at any time is really handy. This system will feature an interface to manage orders, send notifications, and also handle incoming texts asking about orders.

Getting Ready

The complete source code for this recipe can be found in the `Chapter6/Recipe5` folder.

How to do it...

We're now going to build a handy order-tracking system. We'll start with the interface to manage orders and continue onto handling requests for order status. We'll also set up a listener file that will accept SMS messages and reply with the status of the order.

1. Download the Twilio Helper Library from `https://github.com/twilio/twilio-php/zipball/master` and unzip it.

2. Upload the `Services/` folder to your website.

3. Open `sql.sql` and load it to your database.

4. Upload `config.php` to your website and make sure the following variables are set:

```php
<?php
$accountsid = '';    //  YOUR TWILIO ACCOUNT SID
$authtoken = '';     //  YOUR TWILIO AUTH TOKEN
$fromNumber = '';    //  PHONE NUMBER CALLS WILL COME FROM
$dbhost = '';  //  YOUR DATABASE HOST
$dbname = '';  //  YOUR DATABASE NAME
$dbuser = '';  //  YOUR DATABASE USER
$dbpass = '';  //  YOUR DATABASE PASS

$statusArray = array(
'shipped'=>'Shipped',
'fullfillment'=>'Sent to Fullfillment',
'processing'=>'Processing');
?>
```

5. Upload a file called `orders.php` to your server as follows:

```php
<?php
  include('Services/Twilio.php');
  include("config.php");
  include("pdo.class.php");
include("functions.php");

  $client = new Services_Twilio($accountsid, $authtoken);

  $action = isset($_REQUEST['action']) ? $_REQUEST['action'] : '';
  switch($action){
        case 'update':
            $oid = $_GET['oid'];
            $status = $_GET['status'];
            $now = time();
```

```
                    $sql = "UPDATE orders SET
                       `status`='{$status}',`order_date`
                       ='{$now}' WHERE ID='{$oid}'";
                    $pdo = Db::singleton();
                    $pdo->exec($sql);
                    $pdo = Db::singleton();
                    $sql = "SELECT * FROM orders where `ID` =
                          '{$oid}'LIMIT 1";
                    $res = $pdo->query( $sql );
                    while( $row = $res->fetch() ){
                             $message = "Your order has been
                             set to ". $statusArray [$status];
                    send_sms($row['phone_number'],$message);
                    }
header("Location: orders.php");
exit;
                    break;
          case 'save':
                    extract($_POST);
                    $now = time();
                    $sql = "INSERT INTO orders SET
                    order_key`='{$name}',`status`='{$status}',`
                    phone_number`='{$phone_number}',`order_date`
                    ='{$now}'";
                    $pdo = Db::singleton();
                    $pdo->exec($sql);
                    header("Location: orders.php");
exit;
                    break;
          case 'addnew':
                    include("form.php");
                    break;
          default:
                    include("home.php");
                    break;
    }
?>
```

The Orders.php file is your order management system. It lets you enter orders, phone numbers, and update the status. When you change the status, we send an SMS message notifying the customer of the change.

6. Upload a file called `home.php` and add the following code to it:

```php
<!DOCTYPE html>
<html>
<head>
<title>Recipe 4 - Chapter 6</title>
</head>
<body>
<a href="orders.php?action=addnew">Add a new order</a><hr />
<h2>Orders</h2>
<table width="100%">width=100%>
<tr>
  <th>Order ID</th>
  <th>Status</th>
  <th>Order Date</th>
</tr>
<?php
  $pdo = Db:singleton();
  $res = $pdo->query("SELECT * FROM orders ORDER BY
                      `ID`");
  while( $row = $res->fetch() ){
?>
        <tr>
          <td><?=$row['order_key']?></td>
          <td><?=$statusArray[ $row['status'] ]; ?></td>
          <td><?=date("m-d-Y ",$row['order_date'])?></td>
          <td>
<a href="orders.php?oid=<?=$row['ID']?>
&status=shipped&action=update">Mark as Shipped</a>
<a href="orders.php?oid=<?=$row['ID']?>
&status=fullfillment&action=update">Mark as In Fullfillment</a>
<a href="orders.php?oid=<?=$row['ID']?>
&status=processing&action=update">Mark as In Processing</a>
          </td>
        </tr>
<?php
  }
?>
  </table>
  <br />
</body>
</html>
```

7. Upload a file called `form.php` and add the following code to it:

```
<!DOCTYPE html>
<html>
<head>
<title>Recipe 4 - Chapter 6</title>
</head>
<body>
<h2>Add an order</h2>
<form method="POST" action="orders.php?action=save">
<table>
<tr>
   <td>Order ID</td>
   td><input type="text" name="name" /></td>
</tr>
<tr>
   <td>Phone Number</td>
   <td><input type="text" name="phone_number" /></td>
</tr>
<tr>
   <td>Order Date</td>
   <td><input type="text" name="timestamp" placeholder="DD/MM/YY
HH:MM"/></td>
</tr>
<tr>
   <td>Order Status</td>
   <td>
      <select name="status">
<?php
foreach($statusArray as $k=>$v){
   echo '<option value="'.$k.'">'.$v.'</option>';
}
?>
      </select>
   </td>
</tr>
</table>
<button type="submit">Save</button>
</form>
</body>
</html>
```

8. Upload a file called `tracking.php` to your server:

```php
<?php
include("config.php");
include("pdo.class.php");
include("functions.php");

if( isset($_POST['Body']) ){
     $phone = $_POST['From'];
     $order_id = strtolower($_POST['Body']);
     $status = order_lookup($order_id);
     print_sms_reply("Your order is currently set at
                    status '".$status."'");
}else{
     print_sms_reply("Please send us your order id
                    and we will look it up ASAP");
}
```

9. Upload a file called `functions.php` and add the following code to it:

```php
<?php

function send_sms($number,$message){
     global $client,$fromNumber;
     $sms = $client->account->sms_messages->create(
          $fromNumber,
          $number,
          $message
     );
     return $sms->sid;
}

function print_sms_reply ($sms_reply){
     echo "<?xml version=\"1.0\" encoding=\"UTF-
          8\"?>\n";
     echo "<Response>\n<Sms>\n";
     echo $sms_reply;
     echo "</Sms></Response>\n";
}

function order_lookup($order_id){
     global $statusArray;
     $pdo = Db::singleton();
```

```
$sql = "SELECT * FROM orders where `ID` =
        '{$order_id}' OR `order_key` =
        '{$order_id}' LIMIT 1";
$res = $pdo->query( $sql );
while( $row = $res->fetch() ){
        return $statusArray[ $row['status'] ];
}
return 'No Order Matching that ID was found';
}
?>
```

10. To have a number point to this script, log in to your Twilio account and point your Twilio phone number to it:

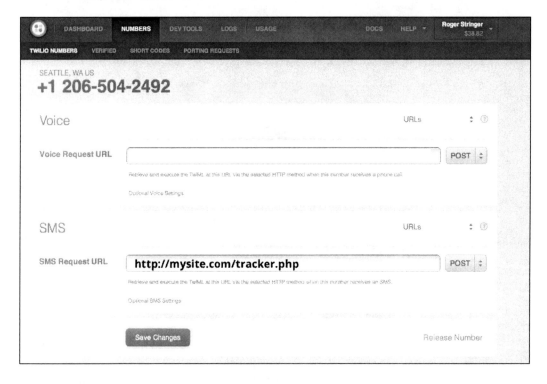

Insert the URL for this page in the **SMS Request URL** box. Then, any text messages that you receive at this number will be processed via `tracking.php`.

How it works...

In steps 1 and 2, we downloaded and installed the Twilio Helper Library for PHP. This library is the heart of your Twilio-powered apps. In step 3, we loaded our database schema into our database.

In step 4, we uploaded `config.php` that contains our authentication information to talk to Twilio's API. In steps 5, 6, and 7, we created our order tracking system. In step 8, we uploaded `tracking.php` that takes all incoming texts.

In step 9, we uploaded `functions.php` that handles our functions that send and receive texts. Finally, in step 10, we told our Twilio number to direct all SMS messages to `tracking.php`.

This recipe has two parts. The first part lets us track our orders and send notifications to customers. The second part replies with a text message whenever the customers sends us a text containing their order ID.

Sending and receiving group chats

Being able to hold a conversation with a group is cool and fun and can be useful for events. This recipe will let you store all conversations for a group in the database and send replies to each member.

Getting ready

The complete source code for this recipe can be found in the `Chapter6/Recipe6/` folder.

How to do it...

We're going to build a simple app that will send and receive messages to and from a group of people. This app will forward any message received at the designated phone number of the people on the group list and send any messages you choose as well.

1. Download the Twilio Helper Library from `https://github.com/twilio/twilio-php/zipball/master` and unzip it.
2. Upload the `Services/` folder to your website.

3. Upload `config.php` to your website and make sure the following variables are set as follows:

```php
<?php
session_start();
$accountsid = '';    //   YOUR TWILIO ACCOUNT SID
$authtoken = '';     //   YOUR TWILIO AUTH TOKEN
$fromNumber = '';    //   PHONE NUMBER CALLS WILL COME FROM

$people = array(
  "+14158675309" => "Curious George",
  "+14158675310" => "Boots",
  "+14158675311" => "Virgil",
);
?>
```

4. Upload a file called `functions.php` and add the following code to it:

```php
<?php
function send_sms($number,$message){
  global $client,$fromNumber;
  $sms = $client->account->sms_messages->create(
          $fromNumber,
          $number,
          $message
  );
  return $sms->sid;
}
function print_sms_reply ($sms_reply){
  echo "<?xml version=\"1.0\" encoding=\"UTF-8\"?>\n";
  echo "<Response>\n<Sms>\n";
  echo $sms_reply;
  echo "</Sms></Response>\n";
}
```

5. Upload a file called `sms.php` to your server as follows:

```php
<!DOCTYPE html>
<html>
<head>
<title>Recipe 5 - Chapter 6</title>
</head>
<body>
<?php
include('Services/Twilio.php');
```

```php
include("config.php");
$client = new Services_Twilio($accountsid, $authtoken);
include("functions.php");

if( isset($_POST['message']) ){
  foreach ($people as $number => $name) {
      $sid = send_sms($number,$_POST['message']);
  }
}
?>
<form method="post">
<input type="text" name="message" placeholder="Message...." /><br
/>
<button type="submit">Send Message</button>
</form>
</body>
</html>
```

6. Upload a file called `listener.php` to your server:

```php
<?php
include("config.php");
$client = new Services_Twilio($accountsid, $authtoken);
include("functions.php");


if( isset($_POST['Body']) ){
  $sid = $_POST['SmsSid'];
  $phone = $_POST['From'];
  $phone = str_replace('+','',$phone);
  $message = strtolower($_POST['Body']);
  $name = $people[ $phone ];
  if( empty($name) )    $name = $phone;
  $message = '['.$name.'] '.$message;
  foreach ($people as $number => $name) {
          if( $number == $phone )    continue;
          $sid = send_sms($number,$message);
  }
  print_sms_reply("Message delivered");
}
?>
```

7. Finally, we have to point your Twilio phone number to it:

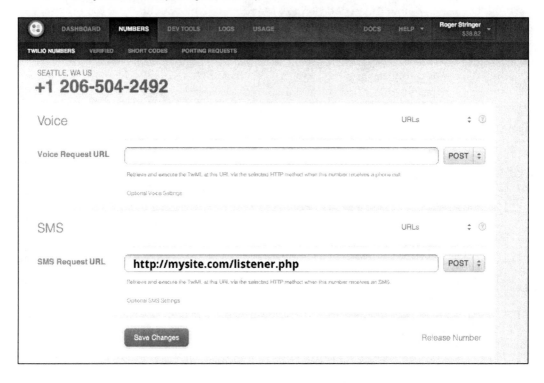

Insert the URL for this page in the **SMS Request URL** box. Then, any calls that you receive at this number will be processed via `listener.php`.

How it works...

In steps 1 and 2, we downloaded and installed the Twilio Helper Library for PHP; this library is the heart of your Twilio-powered apps. In step 3, we uploaded `config.php` that contains our authentication information to talk to Twilio's API.

In step 4, we set up the initial file to send messages. In step 5, we uploaded `sms.php` to the server. Step 6 saw us create the listener and finally step 7 saw us point our Twilio number to `listener.php`.

The group is stored in `config.php`. When we send a message either from `sms.php` or as a reply, it forwards the message to all members of the group.

Sending SMS messages in a phone call

We've handled all other sorts of SMS messages, but what about sending an SMS during a phone call? This recipe will send an SMS message to anyone who calls our phone number.

Getting ready

The complete source code for this recipe can be found in the `Chapter6/Recipe7/` folder.

How to do it...

This recipe will show you how to build a simple app that will send an SMS to the person who called your phone number.

1. Upload `sms.php` to your server as follows:

```php
<?php
  $people = array(
        "+14158675309"=>"Curious George",
        "+14158675310"=>"Boots",
        "+14158675311"=>"Virgil"
  );
  if(!$name = $people[$_REQUEST['From']]) {
        $name = "Monkey";
  }
  header("content-type: text/xml");
  echo "<?xml version=\"1.0\" encoding=\"UTF-8\"?>\n";
?>
<Response>
    <Say>Hello <?php echo $name ?>.</Say>
    <Sms><?php echo $name ?>, thanks for the call!</Sms>
</Response>
```

2. Finally, you have to point your Twilio phone number to it:

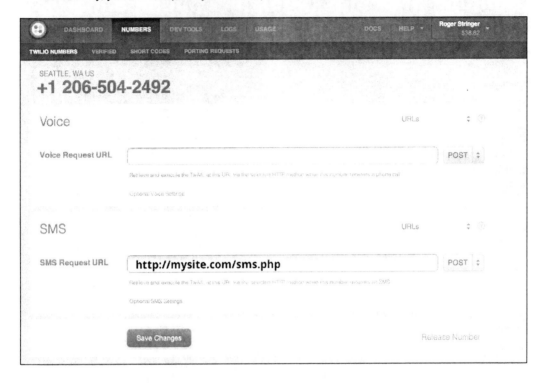

Insert the URL for this page in the **SMS Request URL** box. Then, any calls that you receive at this number will be processed via sms.php.

How it works...

In step 1, we created sms.php. In step 2, we pointed our Twilio phone number to sms.php.

Now, whenever we receive a call, it will check to see if it already knows the caller from their phone number; if so, it will send them a message by name. Otherwise, it will call them Monkey and send them a generic SMS message.

Monitoring a website

I own nearly twenty websites; if those sites go down, my clients get mad. This recipe is a handy recipe to monitor a list of websites every five minutes and, if the site is unreachable, send out a text message.

We're going to use a simple key-value pair datastore system that will store the URL and the current status of the site in a file. If the site is down, we will send a notification to a list of users. Then, if the site is back up the next time the script runs, we will send another notification to the users to tell them that the site is up.

Getting ready

The complete source code for this recipe can be found in the `Chapter6/Recipe8/` folder.

How to do it...

This recipe will build a simple website monitor that we will set up to check a list of sites every five minutes.

1. Download the Twilio Helper Library from `https://github.com/twilio/twilio-php/zipball/master` and unzip it.

2. Upload the `Services/` folder to your website.

3. Upload `config.php` to your website and make sure the following variables are set:

```php
<?php
session_start();
$accountsid = '';    //   YOUR TWILIO ACCOUNT SID
$authtoken = '';     //   YOUR TWILIO AUTH TOKEN
$fromNumber = '';    //   PHONE NUMBER CALLS WILL COME FROM

$people = array(
  "+14158675309" => "Curious George",
  "+14158675310" => "Boots",
  "+14158675311" => "Virgil",
);

$sites = array(
  "http://google.com"=> "Google",
  "http://yahoo.com"=>"Yahoo",
  "http://starbucks.com"=>"Star Bucks"
);
?>
```

4. Upload `datastore.class.php` to your web server.

5. Upload a file called `functions.php` and add the following code to it:

```php
<?php
function check_site($url){
  if( !filter_var($url, FILTER_VALIDATE_URL) ){
    return false;
```

```
  }
  $cl = curl_init($url);
  curl_setopt($cl,CURLOPT_CONNECTTIMEOUT,10);
  curl_setopt($cl,CURLOPT_HEADER,true);
  curl_setopt($cl,CURLOPT_NOBODY,true);
  curl_setopt($cl,CURLOPT_RETURNTRANSFER,true);
  $response = curl_exec($cl);
  curl_close($cl);
  if ($response) return true;
  return false;
  }

  function send_sms($number,$message){
    global $client,$fromNumber;
    $sms = $client->account->sms_messages->create(
            $fromNumber,
            $number,
            $message
    );
    return $sms->sid;
  }
```

6. Upload a file called check.php to your server as follows:

```
<?php
include('Services/Twilio.php');
include("config.php");
include("datastore.class.php");
include("functions.php");

$client = new Services_Twilio($accountsid, $authtoken);
$datastore = new DataStore('check_sites');

foreach($sites as $url=>$name){
  if( !check_site($url) ){
      $datastore->Set($url,'down',0);
      $message = "Oops! The site found at {$url} seems
      to be down!";
      foreach($people as $number=>$person){
              send_sms($number,$message);
      }
  }else{
      $last = $datastore->Get($url);
      if( $last == 'down' ){
```

```
        $message = "Yay! The site found at {$url}
        seems to be back up!";
        foreach($people as $number=>$person){
                send_sms($number,$message);
        }
    }
    $datastore->Set($url,'up',0);
  }
}
```

7. Now, let's set up a cron job to run every five minutes.

```
*/5 * * * * /usr/bin/curl -I "http://www.mywebsite.com/check.php"
```

How it works...

In steps 1 and 2, we downloaded and installed the Twilio Helper Library for PHP. This library is the heart of your Twilio-powered apps and lets us talk to Twilio. In step 3, we uploaded `config.php` that contains our authentication information to talk to Twilio's API.

In step 4, we uploaded `datastore.class.php`, which is a simple key/pair datastore that lets us store a URL and the status of the site. In step 5, we uploaded `functions.php`, which handles checking the status of websites and sending messages when sites are down.

In step 6, we uploaded `check.php`, which loops through our list of sites and sends a notification if a site is down. In step 7, we set up a cron job to check this every five minutes.

Now, if `check.php` is run and a site is down, it notifies the people on the contact list. When it runs again and finds that the site is reachable but was down the last time it ran, we notify the people on the contact list again.

We're using a simple file-based datastore system for this one as a full database isn't necessary. The `datastore` class will create a folder called `_cache` and will store each file as an MD5 hash with the extension of `.store`. So, if a site was called `http://google.com`, the `datastore` file would be `c7b920f57e553df2bb68272f61570210.store`.

7

Building a Reminder System

In this chapter you will learn the following:

- ▶ Scheduling reminders via text messages
- ▶ Getting notified when the time comes
- ▶ Retrieving a list of upcoming reminders
- ▶ Cancelling an upcoming reminder
- ▶ Adding another person to a reminder

Introduction

Being able to set reminders is a handy feature. I find myself setting reminders for just about everything, and this tool has served me well for a couple of years now.

When we're finished, we're going to have a nice reminder system that can be commanded using simple text messages:

- ▶ `Change tires - 11/11/13 @ 11a.m.`: This will set a reminder to get my tires changed on November 11 at 11 a.m.
- ▶ `showme`: This will list all pending reminders.
- ▶ `change tires - cancel`: This will cancel the tire change reminder.
- ▶ `change tires - add 2501121212`: This will add another person to my reminder.

This reminder system is simple, handy, and nice to keep around.

Scheduling reminders via text

This reminder system will let us send a text and get a reminder an hour before it's scheduled.

First, we have to set up the code to actually receive reminders.

Getting ready

The complete source code for this recipe can be found in the `Chapter7/Recipe1` folder

How to do it...

To start with, we're going to build a method to schedule reminders via text messages. We'll build a web app that will let us send a message with a time and save the reminder for later.

1. Download Twilio Helper Library from `https://github.com/twilio/twilio-php/zipball/master` and unzip it.

2. Upload the `Services/` folder to your website.

3. Upload `sql.sql` to your database.

4. Upload `config.php` to your website and make sure the following variables are set:

```php
<?php
  session_start();
  $accountsid = ''; //YOUR TWILIO ACCOUNT SID
  $authtoken = ''; //YOUR TWILIO AUTH TOKEN
  $fromNumber = ''; //    PHONE NUMBER CALLS WILL COME FROM

  $dbhost = ''; //YOUR DATABASE HOST
  $dbname = ''; //YOUR DATABASE NAME
  $dbuser = ''; //YOUR DATABASE USER
  $dbpass = ''; //YOUR DATABASE PASS
?>
```

5. Upload a file called `listener.php` using the following code:

```php
<?php
include('Services/Twilio.php');
include("config.php");
include("functions.php");

if( isset($_POST['Body']) ){
  $phone = $_POST['From'];
  $body = $_POST['Body'];
  $body = strtolower( $body );
```

```php
$keywords = explode(" ",$body);
$key = $keywords[0];
unset( $keywords[0] );
$keywords = implode(" ",$keywords);
$key = strtolower( $key );
$timestamp = strtotime( $action );
//actions
if( $key == 'showme' ){
}else{
  $reminder = explode(' - ',$body);
  $msg = $reminder[0];
  $action = $reminder[1];
  $actions = explode(" ",$action);
  if( $actions[0] == 'cancel' ){
  }else if( $actions[0] == 'add' ){
  }else{
    //new reminder
    $timestamp = strtotime( $action );
    $sql = "INSERT INTO reminders SET
      `message`='{$msg}', `timestamp`='{$timestamp}',
      `phone_number`='{$phone}'";
    $pdo = Db::singleton();
    $pdo->exec($sql);
    $qid = $pdo->lastInsertId();
    print_sms_reply("Your reminder has been set.");
  }
}
//    end actions
}
```

6. Upload a file called `functions.php`:

```php
<?php
function print_sms_reply ($sms_reply){($sms_reply){
  echo "<?xml version=\"1.0\" encoding=\"UTF-8\"?>\n";
  echo "<Response>\n";
  if( !is_array($sms_reply) ){
    echo '<Sms>'.$sms_reply.'</Sms>';
  }else{
    $cnt = count($sms_reply);
    $i = 1;
    foreach($sms_reply as $line){
      $line = $line." (".$i."/".$cnt.")";
      echo '<Sms>'.$line.'</Sms>';
      $i++;
```

```
    }
  }
  echo "</Response>\n";
}
```

7. Finally, you have to point your Twilio phone number to it.

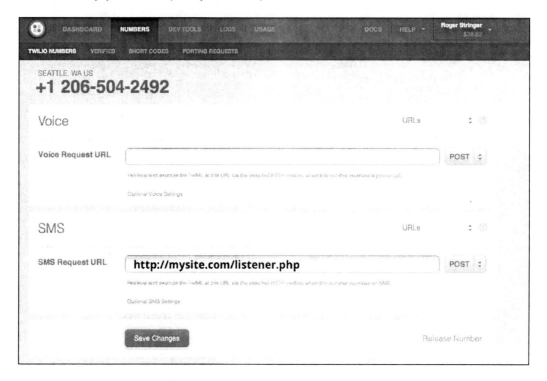

8. Insert `http://mysite.com/listener.php` to this page in the **SMS Request URL** field. Then, any calls that you receive at this number will be processed via `listener.php`.

How it works...

In steps 1 and 2, we downloaded and installed the Twilio Helper Library for PHP; this library is at the heart of your Twilio-powered apps.

In step 3, we loaded our database schema into our database.

In step 4, we uploaded `config.php` that contains our authentication information to communicate with Twilio's API.

In step 5, we uploaded `listener.php` that records all incoming texts.

In step 6, we uploaded `functions.php` that handles any functions we'll use.

In step 7, we informed our Twilio number to direct all SMS messages to `listener.php`.

Now, when we receive a text, we store it as a reminder with the message, timestamp, and the phone number to send it.

Getting notified when the time comes

Ok, we're done adding reminders; now, how do we get reminded? Simple, a cron job that runs each hour and notifies us of upcoming reminders an hour before they are due.

Getting ready

The complete source code for this recipe can be found in the `Chapter7/Recipe2` folder.

How to do it...

Now we're building the part of our reminder system that notifies us when the time comes for the reminder.

1. Download the Twilio Helper Library from `https://github.com/twilio-php/zipball/master` and unzip it.

2. Upload the `Services/` folder to your website.

3. Upload `sql.sql` to your database.

4. Upload `config.php` to your website and make sure the following variables are set:

    ```php
    <?php
      session_start();
      $accountsid = '';//YOUR TWILIO ACCOUNT SID
      $authtoken = '';//YOUR TWILIO AUTH TOKEN
      $fromNumber = '';//PHONE NUMBER CALLS WILL COME FROM

      $dbhost = '';//YOUR DATABASE HOST
      $dbname = '';//YOUR DATABASE NAME
      $dbuser = '';//YOUR DATABASE USER
      $dbpass = '';//YOUR DATABASE PASS
    ?>
    ```

5. Upload `cron.php` to your web server using the following code:

    ```php
    <?php
    include("config.php");
    include("pdo.class.php");
    ```

```
include 'Services/Twilio.php';

$pdo = Db::singleton();
$client = new Services_Twilio($accountsid, $authtoken);

$curtime = strtotime("+1 hour");
$curtime2 = strtotime("+2 hour");
$sql = "SELECT * FROM reminders where (`timestamp` BETWEEN
  $curtime AND $curtime2) AND `notified` = 0";

$res = $pdo->query( $sql );
while( $row = $res->fetch() ){
  $msg = "Reminder: ".$row['message']. ' @ '.date('h:i
    A',$row['timestamp']);;
  $pdo->exec("UPDATE reminders SET `notified` =
    1,`status`=1 WHERE `ID`='{$row['ID']}';");
  $ph = $row['phone_number'];
  $ph2 = $row['phone_number2'];
  $client->account->sms_messages->create( $fromNumber, $ph, $msg
);
  if( !empty($ph2) ){
    $client->account->sms_messages->create( $fromNumber, $ph2,
$msg );
  }
}
```

6. Set `cron.php` to run on an hourly cron as follows:

```
0 * * * * /usr/bin/curl -I
  "http://www.mywebsite.com/cron.php"
```

How it works...

In steps 1 and 2, we downloaded and installed the Twilio Helper Library for PHP; this library is at the heart of your Twilio-powered apps.

In step 3, we loaded our database schema into our database.

In step 4, we uploaded `config.php` that contains our authentication information to communicate with Twilio's API.

In step 5, we uploaded `cron.php`, and in step 6, we set it up to run hourly.

First, we populate the $curtime variable with whatever the time will be one hour from the present. Then we grab all the reminders that are due for that time and send a text message about it.

Retrieving a list of upcoming reminders

Now we will learn how to retrieve a list of upcoming reminders. This will work by sending a text with the message showme; it will send us a list of pending reminders based on phone number.

We're going to build on the first listener.php file by changing the code inside the //actions and //end actions blocks.

Getting ready

The complete source code for this recipe can be found in the Chapter7/Recipe3 folder.

How to do it...

This recipe will extend listener.php to allow us to also return a list of upcoming reminders:

1. Download the Twilio Helper Library from https://github.com/twilio/twilio-php/zipball/master and unzip it.

2. Upload the Services/ folder to your website.

3. Upload sql.sql to your database.

4. Upload config.php to your website and make sure the following variables are set:

```php
<?php
  session_start();
  $accountsid = '';//YOUR TWILIO ACCOUNT SID
  $authtoken = '';//YOUR TWILIO AUTH TOKEN
  $fromNumber = '';//PHONE NUMBER CALLS WILL COME FROM

  $dbhost = '';//YOUR DATABASE HOST
  $dbname = '';//YOUR DATABASE NAME
  $dbuser = '';//YOUR DATABASE USER
  $dbpass = '';//YOUR DATABASE PASS
?>
```

5. Create listener.php as follows:

```php
<?php
include('Services/Twilio.php');
include("config.php");
include("functions.php");

if( isset($_POST['Body']) ){
  $phone = $_POST['From'];
  $body = $_POST['Body'];
```

```
      $from = $_POST['FromCity'].', '.$_POST['FromState'];
      $body = strtolower( $body );
      $keywords = explode(" ",$body);
      $key = $keywords[0];
      unset( $keywords[0] );
      $keywords = implode(" ",$keywords);
      $key = strtolower( $key );
  //actions
      if( $key == 'showme' ){
        $lines = array();
        $curtime = strtotime("+1 hour");
        $sql = "SELECT * FROM reminders where `timestamp` >
          $curtime AND notified = 0";
        $res = $pdo->query( $sql );
        while( $row = $res->fetch() ){
          $lines[] = $row['message'].' - '.date('d/m/Y @ h:i
            A',$row['timestamp']);
        }
        print_sms_reply ($lines);
      }else{
        $reminder = explode(' - ',$body);
        $msg = $reminder[0];
        $action = $reminder[1];
        $actions = explode(" ",$action);
        if( $actions[0] == 'cancel' ){
        }else if( $actions[0] == 'add' ){
        }else{
          //new reminder
          $timestamp = strtotime( $action );
          $sql = "INSERT INTO reminders SET
            `message`='{$msg}',`timestamp`='{$timestamp}',`
            phone_number`='{$phone}'";
          $pdo = Db::singleton();
          $pdo->exec($sql);
          $qid = $pdo->lastInsertId();
          print_sms_reply("Your reminder has been set.");
        }
      }
  //end actions
  }
```

6. Upload a file called `functions.php` using the following code:

```php
<?php
function print_sms_reply ($sms_reply){($sms_reply){
  echo "<?xml version=\"1.0\" encoding=\"UTF-8\"?>\n";
  echo "<Response>\n";
  if( !is_array($sms_reply) ){
    echo '<Sms>'.$sms_reply.'</Sms>';
  }else{
    $cnt = count($sms_reply);
    $i = 1;
    foreach($sms_reply as $line){
      $line = $line." (".$i."/".$cnt.")";
      echo '<Sms>'.$line.'</Sms>';
      $i++;
    }
  }
  echo "</Response>\n";
}
```

7. Finally, we have to point your Twilio phone number to it.

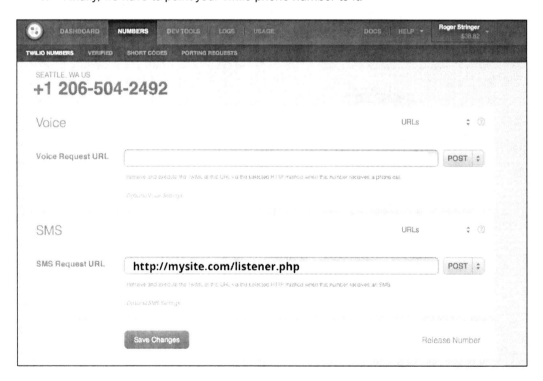

Insert the URL in the **SMS Request URL** field. Then, any calls that you receive at this number will be processed via `listener.php`.

How it works...

In steps 1 and 2, we downloaded and installed the Twilio Helper Library for PHP; this library is at the heart of your Twilio-powered apps.

In step 3, we loaded our database schema into our database.

In step 4, we uploaded `config.php` that contains our authentication information to communicate with Twilio's API.

In steps 5 and 6, we uploaded `listener.php` and `functions.php`, which records all incoming texts.

In step 7, we told our Twilio number to direct all SMS messages to `listener.php`.

When we receive a text, we check it; if it contains the keyword `showme`, we return a list of pending reminders. Otherwise, we add a new reminder to the database.

Canceling an upcoming reminder

Reminders change and sometimes you have to cancel them ahead of time. This recipe will enable the system to handle that.

Getting ready

The complete source code for this recipe can be found in the `Chapter7/Recipe4` folder.

How to do it...

Ok, now we're going to build support for deleting reminders.

1. Download the Twilio Helper Library from `https://github.com/twilio/twilio-php/zipball/master` and unzip it.

2. Upload the `Services/` folder to your website.

3. Upload `sql.sql` to your database

4. Upload `config.php` to your website and make sure the following variables are set:
   ```php
   <?php
     session_start();
     $accountsid = '';//YOUR TWILIO ACCOUNT SID
   ```

```php
$authtoken = '';//YOUR TWILIO AUTH TOKEN
$fromNumber = '';//PHONE NUMBER CALLS WILL COME FROM


$dbhost = '';//YOUR DATABASE HOST
$dbname = '';//YOUR DATABASE NAME
$dbuser = '';//YOUR DATABASE USER
$dbpass = '';//YOUR DATABASE PASS
?>
```

5. Upload a file called `listener.php` with the help of the following code:

```php
<?php
include('Services/Twilio.php');
include("config.php");
include("functions.php");

if( isset($_POST['Body']) ){
  $phone = $_POST['From'];
  $body = $_POST['Body'];
  $from = $_POST['FromCity'].', '.$_POST['FromState'];
  $body = strtolower( $body );
  $keywords = explode(" ",$body);
  $key = $keywords[0];
  unset( $keywords[0] );
  $keywords = implode(" ",$keywords);
  $key = strtolower( $key );
//actions
  if( $key == 'showme' ){
    $lines = array();
    $curtime = strtotime("+1 hour");
    $sql = "SELECT * FROM reminders where `timestamp` >  $curtime
      AND notified = 0";
    $res = $pdo->query( $sql );
    while( $row = $res->fetch() ){
      $lines[] = $row['message'].' - '.date('d/m/Y @ h:i
        A',$row['timestamp']);
    }
    print_sms_reply ($lines);
  }else{
    $reminder = explode(' - ',$body);
    $msg = $reminder[0];
```

```php
      $action = $reminder[1];
      $actions = explode(" ",$action);
      if( $actions[0] == 'cancel' ){
        $pdo = Db::singleton();
        $pdo->exec("DELETE reminders WHERE `message`='{$msg}'
          AND `phone_number`='{$phone}';");
        print_sms_reply("Your reminder has been cancelled.");
      }else if( $actions[0] == 'add' ){
      }else{
        //new reminder
        $timestamp = strtotime( $action );
        $sql = "INSERT INTO reminders SET `message`='{$msg}',`timest
amp`='{$timestamp}',`phone_number`='{$phone
  }'";
        $pdo = Db::singleton();
        $pdo->exec($sql);
        $qid = $pdo->lastInsertId();
        print_sms_reply("Your reminder has been set.");
      }
    }
//end actions
}
```

6. Upload a file called `functions.php` with the following code:

```php
<?php
function print_sms_reply ($sms_reply){($sms_reply){
  echo "<?xml version=\"1.0\" encoding=\"UTF-8\"?>\n";
  echo "<Response>\n";
  if( !is_array($sms_reply) ){
    echo '<Sms>'.$sms_reply.'</Sms>';
  }else{
    $cnt = count($sms_reply);
    $i = 1;
    foreach($sms_reply as $line){
      $line = $line." (".$i."/".$cnt.")";
      echo '<Sms>'.$line.'</Sms>';
      $i++;
    }
  }
  echo "</Response>\n";
}
```

7. Finally, you have to point your Twilio phone number to it.

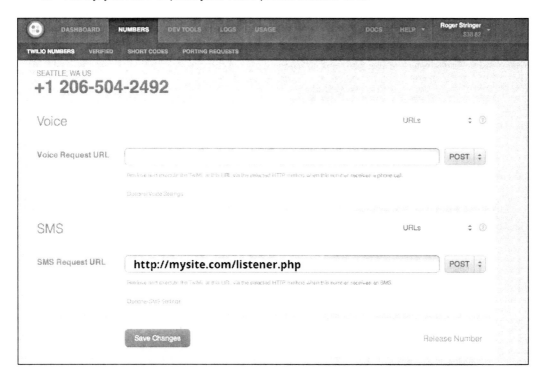

Insert `http://mysite.com/listener.php` in the **SMS Request URL** field. Then, any calls that you receive at this number will be processed via `listener.php`.

How it works...

In steps 1 and 2, we downloaded and installed the Twilio Helper Library for PHP; this library is at the heart of your Twilio-powered apps.

In step 3, we loaded our database schema into our database.

In step 4, we uploaded `config.php` that contains our authentication information to communicate with Twilio's API.

In steps 5 and 6, we uploaded `listener.php` and `functions.php`, which records all incoming texts.

In step 7, we told our Twilio number to direct all SMS messages to `listener.php`.

When we receive a text, we check it; if it contains the keyword `showme`, we return a list of pending reminders.

Then we check to see if the `cancel` keyword was sent with the reminder.

So `change tires - cancel` would check for a pending reminder with my phone number and the message of "change tires" and delete it.

Adding another person to a reminder

I first had to add this functionality when adding my wife to reminders. It's worked well for me since, so here it is.

Getting ready

The complete source code for this recipe can be found in the `Chapter7/Recipe5` folder.

How to do it...

Let's add another person to our reminders. We're going to add the ability to add a second phone number to a reminder and have them get notified when you get notified.

1. Download the Twilio Helper Library from `https://github.com/twilio/twilio-php/zipball/master` and unzip it.

2. Upload the `Services/` folder to your website.

3. Upload `sql.sql` to your database

4. Upload `config.php` to your website and make sure the following variables are set:

    ```php
    <?php
    session_start();
    $accountsid = '';//YOUR TWILIO ACCOUNT SID
        $authtoken = '';//YOUR TWILIO AUTH TOKEN
        $fromNumber = '';//PHONE NUMBER CALLS WILL COME FROM

        $dbhost = '';//YOUR DATABASE HOST
        $dbname = '';//YOUR DATABASE NAME
        $dbuser = '';//YOUR DATABASE USER
        $dbpass = '';//YOUR DATABASE PASS
    ?>
    ```

5. Upload a file called `listener.php` using the following code:

```php
<?php
include('Services/Twilio.php');
include("config.php");
include("functions.php");

if( isset($_POST['Body']) ){
  $phone = $_POST['From'];
  $body = $_POST['Body'];
  $from = $_POST['FromCity'].', '.$_POST['FromState'];
  $body = strtolower( $body );
  $keywords = explode(" ",$body);
  $key = $keywords[0];
  unset( $keywords[0] );
  $keywords = implode(" ",$keywords);
  $key = strtolower( $key );
//actions
  if( $key == 'showme' ){
    $lines = array();
    $curtime = strtotime("+1 hour");
    $sql = "SELECT * FROM reminders where `timestamp` >  $curtime
      AND notified = 0";
    $res = $pdo->query( $sql );
    while( $row = $res->fetch() ){
      $lines[] = $row['message'].' - '.date('d/m/Y @ h:i
        A',$row['timestamp']);
    }
    print_sms_reply ($lines);
  }else{
    $reminder = explode(' - ',$body);
    $msg = $reminder[0];
    $action = $reminder[1];
    $actions = explode(" ",$action);
    if( $actions[0] == 'cancel' ){
      $pdo = Db::singleton();
      $pdo->exec("DELETE reminders WHERE `message`='{$msg}'
        AND `phone_number`='{$phone}';");
      print_sms_reply("Your reminder has been cancelled.");
    }else if( $actions[0] == 'add' ){
      //second phone number from $actions[1]
      $pdo = Db::singleton();
```

```
            $pdo->exec("UPDATE reminders SET
                `phone_number2`='{$actions[1]}' WHERE `message`='{$msg}'
               AND `phone_number`='{$phone}';");
            print_sms_reply("Your reminder has been updated.");
        }else{
            //new reminder
            $timestamp = strtotime( $action );
            $sql = "INSERT INTO reminders SET
                `message`='{$msg}',`timestamp`='{$timestamp}',`phone_
number`=
               '{$phone}'";
            $pdo = Db::singleton();
            $pdo->exec($sql);
            $qid = $pdo->lastInsertId();
            print_sms_reply("Your reminder has been set.");
        }
    }
    //end actions
}
```

6. Upload a file called functions.php in accordance with the following code:

```php
<?php
function print_sms_reply ($sms_reply){($sms_reply){
  echo "<?xml version=\"1.0\" encoding=\"UTF-8\"?>\n";
  echo "<Response>\n";
  if( !is_array($sms_reply) ){
    echo '<Sms>'.$sms_reply.'</Sms>';
  }else{
    $cnt = count($sms_reply);
    $i = 1;
    foreach($sms_reply as $line){
      $line = $line." (".$i."/".$cnt.")";
      echo '<Sms>'.$line.'</Sms>';
      $i++;
    }
  }
  echo "</Response>\n";
}
```

7. Finally, you have to point your Twilio phone number to it.

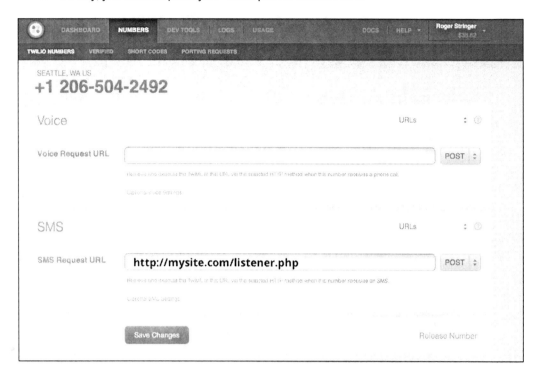

8. Insert `http://mysite.com/listener.php` to this page in the **SMS Request URL** field. Then, any calls that you receive at this number will be processed via `listener.php`.

How it works...

In steps 1 and 2, we downloaded and installed the Twilio Helper Library for PHP; this library is at the heart of your Twilio-powered apps.

In step 3, we loaded our database schema into our database.

In step 4, we uploaded `config.php`, which contains our authentication information to communicate with Twilio's API.

In steps 5 and 6, we uploaded `listener.php` and `functions.php`, which records all incoming texts.

In step 7, we told our Twilio number to direct all SMS messages to `listener.php`.

When we receive a text, we check it; if it contains the keyword `showme`, we return a list of pending reminders.

Then we check to see if the `cancel` keyword was sent with the reminder.

So `change tires - cancel` would check for a pending reminder with my phone number and the message of `change tires` and delete it.

Our final action is to check if we are adding a second phone number to the reminder. If we pass the reminder with `add 1112223344`, we would add the phone number to the reminder.

So `change tires - cancel` would check for a pending reminder with my phone number and the message of `change tires` and delete it.

8
Building an IVR System

In this chapter, you will learn the following recipes:

- ► Setting up IVRs
- ► Screening and recording calls
- ► Logging and reporting calls
- ► Looking up HighriseHQ contacts on incoming calls
- ► Getting directions
- ► Leaving a message
- ► Sending an SMS to your Salesforce.com contacts

Introduction

IVRs, **Interactive Voice Response systems**, are automated phone systems that can facilitate communication between callers and businesses. If you have ever been able to get through to your bank to check balance after responding to a series of automated prompts, you have used an IVR.

Businesses use IVR systems for a number of purposes, such as:

- ► Answering a call and prompting menu options for the caller to choose
- ► Directing the call to an agent, such as sales or support
- ► Acting as a voicemail or an answering machine

Taking it a step further, IVR systems are heavily in use for services such as:

▸ Mobile: Pay-as-you-go account funding; registration; and mobile purchases such as ringtones and logos

▸ Banking: balance, payments, transfers, transaction history, and so on

▸ Retail and Entertainment: orders, bookings, credit and debit card payments

▸ Utilities: meter readings

▸ Travel: ticket booking, flight information, checking in, and so on

▸ Weather forecasts: water, road, and ice conditions

Using PHP and the Twilio API, you can easily create a powerful IVR for your business.

In this chapter, we will set up a basic IVR system, perform call screening and recording, log and report the calls, and also check our incoming calls to see whether they exist in our Highrise CRM account.

We'll also show you how to add extra options on to your IVR menu by adding the ability to get directions to the office.

Finally, we will set up a system to get a list of contacts from our `www.Salesforce.com` account and send an SMS to them.

Setting up IVRs

In this first section, we will set up our basic IVR with a simple phone tree.

When a caller calls in, we'll give them a list of options. Pressing 1 will give them the store hours, and pressing 2 will prompt them to enter the extension of an agent.

Getting ready

The complete source code for this recipe can be found in the `Chapter8/Recipe1/` folder

How to do it...

Let's set up the basic IVR system. The basic system will consist of a simple company directory, which would display the incoming calls.

When a user calls in, it will greet them and then prompt them to make a choice.

1. Upload `config.php` on your website and make sure your phone tree variables are set:

```php
<?php
  $directory = array(
```

```php
      '1'=> array(
        'phone'=>'415-555-2222',
        'firstname' => 'Joe',
        'lastname' => 'Doe'
      ),
      '2'=> array(
        'phone'=>'415-555-3333',
        'firstname' => 'Eric',
        'lastname' => 'Anderson'
      ),
      '3'=> array(
        'phone'=>'415-555-4444',
        'firstname' => 'John',
        'lastname' => 'Easton'
      ),
    );
```

2. Upload a file called `listener.php`:

```php
<?php
  header('Content-type: text/xml');
  echo '<?xml version="1.0" encoding="UTF-8"?>';
?>
<Response>
  <Gather action="input.php" numDigits="1">
    <Say>Welcome to my pretend company.</Say>
    <Say>For store hours, press 1.</Say>
    <Say>To speak to an agent, press 2.</Say>
  </Gather>
  <!-- If customer doesn't input anything, prompt and try
    again. -->
  <Say>Sorry, I didn't get your response.</Say>
  <Redirect>listener.php</Redirect>
</Response>
```

Listener is the first responder; it's called when a caller first calls our phone number, and from there we send the caller to the next file.

`Listener.php` contains our initial menu options, and it prompts the caller to make a decision.

3. Now, create a file called `input.php` as follows:

```php
<?php
  header('Content-type: text/xml');
  echo '<?xml version="1.0" encoding="UTF-8"?>';
  echo '<Response>';
```

```php
      $user_pushed = (int) $_REQUEST['Digits'];
      switch( $user_pushed ){
        case 1:
          echo '<Say>Our store hours are 8 AM to 8 PM
            everyday.</Say>';
          break;
        case 2:
          echo '<Gather action="extensions.php"
            numDigits="1">';
          echo "<Say>Please enter your party's
            extension.</Say>";
          echo '<Say>Press 0 to return to the main menu</Say>';
          echo '</Gather>';
          echo "<Say>Sorry, I didn't get your response.</Say>";
          echo '<Redirect method="GET">input.php?Digits=2
            </Redirect>';
          break;
        default:
          echo "<Say>Sorry, I can't do that yet.</Say>";
          echo '<Redirect>listener.php</Redirect>';
          break;
      }
      echo '</Response>';
  ?>
```

4. The last file to be created is `extensions.php` as follows:

```php
  <?php
    include("config.php");
    header('Content-type: text/xml');
    echo '<?xml version="1.0" encoding="UTF-8"?>';
    echo '<Response>';
    $user_pushed = (int) $_REQUEST['Digits'];
    switch( $user_pushed ){
      case 0:
        echo '<Say>Taking you back to the main menu</Say>';
        echo '<Redirect>listener.php</Redirect>';
        break;
      default:
        if( isset( $directory[$user_pushed] ) ){
          $agent = $directory[$user_pushed];
          echo '<Say>Connecting you to '.$agent['firstname'].'.</
Say>';
          echo '<Dial>'.$agent['phone'].'</Dial>';
        }else{
```

```
      echo "<Say>Sorry, that extension is unknown.
        </Say>";
      echo '<Redirect method="GET">input.php?Digits=2
        </Redirect>';
    }
      break;
  }
  echo '</Response>';
?>
```

5. Finally, you have to point your Twilio phone number to the `extensions.php` file:

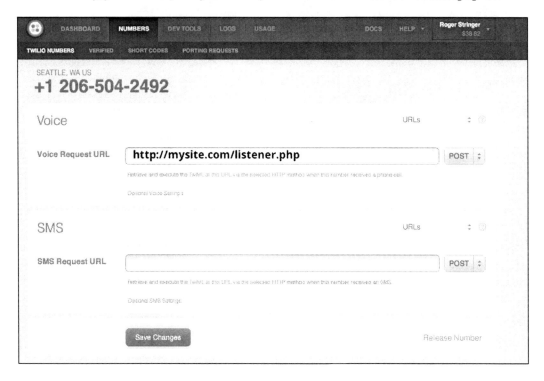

Insert the URL to this page in the **Voice Request URL** field. Then, any calls that you receive at this number will be processed via `listener.php`.

How it works...

In step 1, we uploaded `config.php` that contains our company directory.

In steps 2, 3, and 4, we set up `listener.php`, `input.php`, and `extensions.php` that take the incoming calls, and accept an input from the caller to either return the call during business hours or connect them to an agent.

Finally, we used step 5 to add `listener.php` to a phone number, which means any incoming calls to that phone number go through `listener.php`.

Once a caller calls in, they will be greeted and then prompted to either hit 1 or 2. If they choose 1, we'll give them the store hours and if they hit 2, we'll ask them to enter an extension for an agent to call.

If they press an extension, we then check to see if there is a match and if so, we direct a call to them.

Screening and recording calls

Ok, we've set up a basic IVR. Now let's expand it a little and include the ability for our agents to accept a call or not.

We'll also set it up to record calls, which is standard for most IVR systems.

When calls come in, the agent will be prompted to press 1 to accept the call or, otherwise, any other number to disconnect the call.

Getting ready

The complete source code for this recipe can be found in the `Chapter8/Recipe2/` folder.

How to do it...

This recipe will let us screen and record the calls we take. When a call is connected to an agent, they will receive a prompt whether they want to accept the call or not. If they want to accept it, they will hit 1 and the call will be connected. Pressing any other key will reject the call and hang it up.

1. First, update `extensions.php` as follows:

```php
<?php
  include("config.php");
  header('Content-type: text/xml');
  echo '<?xml version="1.0" encoding="UTF-8"?>';
  echo '<Response>';
  $user_pushed = (int) $_REQUEST['Digits'];
  switch( $user_pushed ){
    case 0:
      echo '<Say>Taking you back to the main menu</Say>';
      echo '<Redirect>listener.php</Redirect>';
      break;
    default:
```

```php
        if( isset( $directory[$user_pushed] ) ){
          $agent = $directory[$user_pushed];
          echo '<Say>Connecting you to '.$agent['firstname']
            .'. All calls are recorded.</Say>';
          echo '<Dial record="true">';
          echo '<Number url="screen-caller.xml">'
            .$agent['phone'].'</Number>';
          echo '</Dial>';
        }else{
          echo "<Say>Sorry, that extension is unknown.
            </Say>";
          echo '<Redirect method="GET">input.php?Digits=2
            </Redirect>';
        }
        break;
    }
    echo '</Response>';
?>
```

2. Now, create a file called `screen-caller.xml`:

```xml
<?xml version="1.0" encoding="UTF-8"?>
<Response>
  <Gather action="screen.php" numDigits="1">
    <Say>You have an incoming call.</Say>
    <Say>To accept the call, press 1.</Say>
    <Say>To reject the call, press any other key.</Say>
  </Gather>
  <!-- If customer doesn't input anything, prompt and
    try again. -->
  <Say>Sorry, I didn't get your response.</Say>
  <Redirect>screen-caller.xml</Redirect>
</Response>
```

3. Finally, let's create a file called `screen.php`:

```php
<?php
  header('Content-type: text/xml');
  echo '<?xml version="1.0" encoding="UTF-8"?>';
  echo '<Response>';
  $user_pushed = (int) $_REQUEST['Digits'];
  switch( $user_pushed ){
    case 1:
      echo '<Say>Connecting you to the caller. All calls
        are recorded.</Say>';
      break;
    default:
```

```
            echo '<Hangup />';
            break;
    }
    echo '</Response>';
?>
```

How it works...

In step 1, we updated `extensions.php`.

In step 2, we created `screen-caller.xml` and in step 3, we created `screen.php`.

This system builds on the original IVR we built in *Chapter 1, Into the Frying Pan*, but changes a few files and adds two new pieces of functionalities.

First, we set the calls to record; we also include a message for the caller indicating that all calls are recorded.

Second, we allow our agent to confirm whether they want to take the call. If the agent presses 1, the call is accepted; otherwise, the call is hung up.

Logging and reporting calls

Another important aspect of IVRs is the ability to log calls. This helps us to go back and see how many calls have come in and when.

When a call comes in, we will store the phone number and the date and time of the call.

We'll also build a basic monitor to view call logs.

Getting ready

The complete source code for this recipe can be found in the `Chapter8/Recipe3/` folder.

How to do it...

Let's set up a simple call logging system that lets us track calls. When a caller calls in, we'll update our database with a log of the call. Then, we'll be able to open a page and view all the calls.

1. Open `sql.sql` and load the schema into your database.

2. Update `config.php` to your website and make sure your phone tree variables are set:

```php
<?php
  $dbhost = '';      //      YOUR DATABASE HOST
  $dbname = '';      //      YOUR DATABASE NAME
  $dbuser = '';      //      YOUR DATABASE USER
$dbpass = ''; //      YOUR DATABASE PASS

   $directory = array(
     '1'=> array(
       'phone'=>'415-555-2222',
       'firstname' => 'Joe',
       'lastname' => 'Doe'
     ),
     '2'=> array(
       'phone'=>'415-555-3333',
       'firstname' => 'Eric',
       'lastname' => 'Anderson'
     ),
     '3'=> array(
       'phone'=>'415-555-4444',
       'firstname' => 'John',
       'lastname' => 'Easton'
      ),
    );
```

3. Update `listener.php` as follows:

```php
<?php
  include("config.php");
  include("pdo.class.php");
  $pdo = Db::singleton();

  $now = time();
  $sql = "INSERT INTO calls SET caller='{$_REQUEST['From']}',
call_time='{$now}'";
  $pdo->exec( $sql );

  header('Content-type: text/xml');
  echo '<?xml version="1.0" encoding="UTF-8"?>';
?>
<Response>
```

```
<Gather action="input.php" numDigits="1">
  <Say>Welcome to my pretend company.</Say>
  <Say>For store hours, press 1.</Say>
  <Say>To speak to an agent, press 2.</Say>
</Gather>
<!-- If customer doesn't input anything, prompt and
  try again. -->
<Say>Sorry, I didn't get your response.</Say>
<Redirect>listener.php</Redirect>
</Response>
```

4. Now create a file called `log.php` as follows:

```php
<?php
  include("config.php");
  include("pdo.class.php");
  $pdo = Db::singleton();

  $result = $pdo->query('SELECT caller, call_time FROM calls');
  echo '<ul>';
  while( $row = $result->fetch() ){
    echo '<li>A call came in on '.date("F j, Y, g:i a",
      $row['call_time']).' from '.$row['caller'].'</li>';
  }
  echo '</ul>';
?>
```

How it works...

In step 1, we set up our database.

In step 2, we updated `config.php` that contains our company directory and our database settings.

In step 3, we updated `listener.php` in order to add incoming calls to our database for tracking purposes.

Finally, in step 4, we created a file called `log.php` that we can use to view a call log of incoming calls.

`Listener.php` works the same as in our previous recipes but it also adds the calls to a table in our database.

If we load `log.php`, we get a nice view of the calls we've had.

Looking up HighriseHQ contacts on incoming calls

I'm using Highrise for this example, as that is the CRM I use. But you can quickly modify this for any CRM.

This IVR integration will check your incoming call and see if the phone number exists in your Highrise contacts. If it does, it will add the caller's name to the database record.

You'll need a Highrise account to do this, and you can get one at `http://highrisehq.com`.

There are two credentials you'll need for this, your account name and your API key.

You can get your account name from the address bar of your browser:

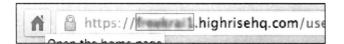

And then, you can find your API key by clicking **My Account** and then going to **API token**:

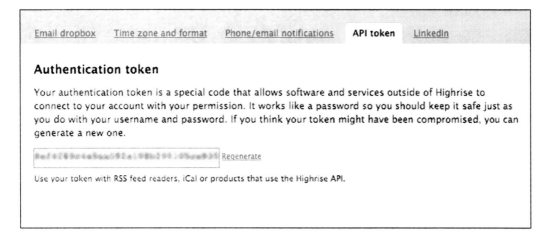

Getting ready

The complete source code for this recipe can be found in the `Chapter8/Recipe4/` folder.

How to do it...

We're going to enhance our IVR system to perform a look-up on our HighriseHQ account and create a log if the caller is known to us. When we view `log.php`, we will see whether the caller was known to us or not from Highrise.

1. Download the PHP Highrise API from `https://github.com/ignaciovazquez/Highrise-PHP-Api/` and upload the `HighRiseAPI.class.php` file to your server in the `Services` folder.

2. Open `sql.sql` and copy the schema to your database.

3. Update `config.php` to your website and make sure your phone tree variables are set:

```php
<?php
  $dbhost = '';//YOUR DATABASE HOST
  $dbname = '';//YOUR DATABASE NAME
  $dbuser = '';//YOUR DATABASE USER
  $dbpass = '';//YOUR DATABASE PASS

  $highrise_account = '';
  $highrise_apikey = '';

  $directory = array(
    '1'=> array(
      'phone'=>'415-555-2222',
      'firstname' => 'Joe',
      'lastname' => 'Doe'
    ),
    '2'=> array(
'phone'=>'415-555-3333',
      'firstname' => 'Eric',
      'lastname' => 'Anderson'
    ),
    '3'=> array(
      'phone'=>'415-555-4444',
      'firstname' => 'John',
      'lastname' => 'Easton'
    ),
  );
```

4. Update `listener.php` as follows:

```php
<?php
  include("config.php");
  include("pdo.class.php");
```

```php
    $pdo = Db::singleton();

    require_once("Services/HighriseAPI.class.php");

    $highrise = new HighriseAPI();
    $highrise->debug = false;
    $highrise->setAccount( $highrise_account );
    $highrise->setToken( $highrise_apikey );

    $people = $highrise->findPeopleBySearchCriteria(
      array('phone'=>$_REQUEST['From'])
    );
    if( count($people) ){
      $p = $people[0];
      $name =$p->getFirstName().' '.$p->getLastName();
      $now = time();
      $sql = "INSERT INTO calls SET caller_
name='{$name}',caller='{$_REQUEST['From']}',
  call_time='{$now}'";
      $pdo->exec( $sql );
    }else{
      $now = time();
      $sql = "INSERT INTO calls SET caller='{$_REQUEST['From']}',
call_time='{$now}'";
      $pdo->exec( $sql );
    }
    header('Content-type: text/xml');
    echo '<?xml version="1.0" encoding="UTF-8"?>';
?>
<Response>
  <Gather action="input.php" numDigits="1">
    <Say>Welcome to my pretend company.</Say>
    <Say>For store hours, press 1.</Say>
    <Say>To speak to an agent, press 2.</Say>
  </Gather>
  <!-- If customer doesn't input anything, prompt and
    try again. -->
  <Say>Sorry, I didn't get your response.</Say>
  <Redirect>listener.php</Redirect>
</Response>
```

5. Now update `log.php` as follows:

```php
<?php
  include("config.php");
  include("pdo.class.php");
  $pdo = Db::singleton();

  $result = $pdo->query('SELECT caller, call_time FROM
    calls');
  echo '<ul>';
  while( $row = $result->fetch() ){
    if( !empty($row['caller_name']) ){
      echo '<li>A call came in on '.date("F j, Y, g:i a",
        $row['call_time']).' from '.$row['caller'].'
('.$row['caller_name'].')</li>';
    }else{
      echo '<li>A call came in on '.date("F j, Y, g:i a",
        $row['call_time']).' from '.$row['caller'].'</li>';
    }
  }
  echo '</ul>';
?>
```

How it works...

In step 1, we download the Highrise API PHP library.

In step 2, we set up our database

In step 3, we uploaded `config.php` that contains our company directory and also our database information and credentials to talk to our Highrise account.

In step 4, we updated `listener.php` to perform a look-up of our Highrise account, based on the incoming phone number, and look for a match. If a match is found, it stores the caller's name in the call log as well as the phone number. Otherwise, it stores the phone number.

In step 5, we updated `log.php` to display the caller's name if it is stored.

We could use other CRMs for this but I'm a heavy Highrise user and use their API quite a lot; so that's why I chose to work with this one here.

Getting directions

Let's expand our IVR menu options a little. We're going to add a new option to let our callers request directions.

This will also demonstrate how to make the menu do more.

This example will set up the IVR menu so that if the caller presses 3, they will be informed of our main office; it will also prompt them to press another key for directions from different locations.

Getting Ready

The complete source code for this recipe can be found in the `Chapter8/Recipe5/` folder.

How to do it...

Let's expand our IVR app to include some more options, such as business directions. We'll also add an option to make our phones quack like a duck just to make it interesting.

1. Update `listener.php` as follows:

```php
<?php
  include("config.php");
  include("pdo.class.php");
  $pdo = Db::singleton();

  require_once("Services/HighriseAPI.class.php");

  $highrise = new HighriseAPI();
  $highrise->debug = false;
  $highrise->setAccount( $highrise_account );
  $highrise->setToken( $highrise_apikey );

  $people = $highrise->findPeopleBySearchCriteria(
    array('phone'=>$_REQUEST['From'])
  );
  if( count($people) ){
    $p = $people[0];
    $name =$p->getFirstName().' '.$p->getLastName();
    $now = time();
    $sql = "INSERT INTO calls SET caller_
name='{$name}',caller='{$_REQUEST['From']}',
      call_time='{$now}'";
    $pdo->exec( $sql );
  }else{
```

```php
    $now = time();
    $sql = "INSERT INTO calls SET caller=
        '{$_REQUEST['From']}', call_time='{$now}'";
    $pdo->exec( $sql );
  }
  header('Content-type: text/xml');
  echo '<?xml version="1.0" encoding="UTF-8"?>';
?>
<Response>
  <Gather action="input.php" numDigits="1">
    <Say>Welcome to my pretend company.</Say>
    <Say>For store hours, press 1.</Say>
    <Say>For directions, press 2</Say>
    <Say>To speak to an agent, press 3.</Say>
    <Say>To speak to a duck, press 4.</Say>
  </Gather>
  <!-- If customer doesn't input anything, prompt and
    try again. -->
  <Say>Sorry, I didn't get your response.</Say>
  <Redirect>listener.php</Redirect>
</Response>
```

2. Update `input.php` as follows:

```php
<?php
  header('Content-type: text/xml');
  echo '<?xml version="1.0" encoding="UTF-8"?>';
  echo '<Response>';
  $user_pushedo = (int) $_REQUEST['Digits'];
  switch( $user_pushed ){
    case 1:
      echo '<Say>Our store hours are 8 AM to 8 PM
        everyday.</Say>';
      break;
    case '2';
      echo '<Say>My pretend company is located at 101 4th
        Street in Neverland</Say>';
      echo '<Gather action="input.php" numDigits="1">';
      echo '<Say>For directions from the First Star to the
        right, press 5</Say>';
      echo '<Say>For directions from San Jose, press
        6</Say>';
      echo '</Gather>';
      echo "<Say>Sorry, I didn't get your response.</Say>";
      echo '<Redirect method="GET">listener.php
        </Redirect>';
```

```php
          break;
     case 3:
       echo '<Gather action="extensions.php"
         numDigits="1">';
       echo "<Say>Please enter your party's extension.
         </Say>";
       echo '<Say>Press 0 to return to the main menu</Say>';
       echo '</Gather>';
       echo "<Say>Sorry, I didn't get your response.</Say>";
       echo '<Redirect method="GET">input.php?Digits=2</Redirect>';
       break;
     case 4:
       echo '<Play>duck.mp3</Play>';
       break;
     case 5:
       echo '<Say>Take the first star to the right and
         follow it straight on to the dawn.</Say>';
       break;
     case 6:
       echo '<Say>Take Cal Train to the Milbrae BART
         station. Take any Bart train to Powell Street
         </Say>';
       break;
     default:
       echo "<Say>Sorry, I can't do that yet.</Say>";
       echo '<Redirect>listener.php</Redirect>';
       break;
   }
   echo '<Pause/>';
   echo '<Say>Main Menu</Say>';
   echo '<Redirect>listener.php</Redirect>';
   echo '</Response>';
 ?>
```

3. Upload a new file called `duck.mp3`.

How it works...

We've just updated `listener.php` and `input.php`.

Now, when a caller calls in, they get a few other options that give them directions to the nearest office. They can also hear a duck quack.

The quack is to demonstrate the `<play>` verb from Twilio instead of just saying words; we can also play any MP3 or WAV file simply by adding the `<play>file.mp3</play>` command into our workflow.

Leaving a message

OK, instead of hanging up the call when an agent doesn't answer, let's forward them to a company voice mailbox.

Getting Ready

The complete source code for this recipe can be found in the `Chapter8/Recipe6/` folder.

How to do it...

We're going to set this up so that, if a caller can't reach an agent, or just generally wants to leave a message, they can do so by pressing 5.

1. Download the Twilio Helper Library from `https://github.com/twilio/twilio-php/zipball/master` and unzip it.

2. Upload the `Services/` folder to your website.

3. Update `config.php` to your website and make sure the following variables are set:

```php
<?php
$dbhost = '';//YOUR DATABASE HOST
$dbname = '';//YOUR DATABASE NAME
$dbuser = '';//YOUR DATABASE USER
$dbpass = '';//YOUR DATABASE PASS

  $highrise_account = '';
  $highrise_apikey = '';


  $accountsid = '';//YOUR TWILIO ACCOUNT SID
  $authtoken = '';//YOUR TWILIO AUTH TOKEN
  $fromNumber = '';//      PHONE NUMBER CALLS WILL
    COME FROM

  $directory = array(
    '1'=> array(
      'phone'=>'415-555-2222',
      'firstname' => 'Joe',
      'lastname' => 'Doe'
    ),
    '2'=> array(
      'phone'=>'415-555-3333',
```

```
                'firstname' => 'Eric',
                'lastname' => 'Anderson'
            ),
        '3'=> array(
                'phone'=>'415-555-4444',
                'firstname' => 'John',
                'lastname' => 'Easton'
            ),
        );
```

4. Update `listener.php` as follows:

```php
<?php
    include("config.php");
    include("pdo.class.php");
    $pdo = Db::singleton();

    require_once("Services/HighriseAPI.class.php");

    $highrise = new HighriseAPI();
    $highrise->debug = false;
    $highrise->setAccount( $highrise_account );
    $highrise->setToken( $highrise_apikey );

    $people = $highrise->findPeopleBySearchCriteria(
        array('phone'=>$_REQUEST['From'])
    );
    if( count($people) ){
        $p = $people[0];
        $name =$p->getFirstName().' '.$p->getLastName();
        $now = time();
        $sql = "INSERT INTO calls SET caller_
name='{$name}',caller='{$_REQUEST['From']}', call_time='{$now}'";
        $pdo->exec( $sql );
    }else{
        $now = time();
        $sql = "INSERT INTO calls SET caller='{$_REQUEST['From']}',
call_time='{$now}'";
        $pdo->exec( $sql );
    }
    header('Content-type: text/xml');
    echo '<?xml version="1.0" encoding="UTF-8"?>';
?>
<Response>
```

```
  <Gather action="input.php" numDigits="1">
    <Say>Welcome to my pretend company.</Say>
    <Say>For store hours, press 1.</Say>
    <Say>For directions, press 2</Say>
    <Say>To speak to an agent, press 3.</Say>
    <Say>To speak to a duck, press 4.</Say>
    <Say>To leave a message, press 5.</Say>
  </Gather>
  <!-- If customer doesn't input anything, prompt and
    try again. -->
  <Say>Sorry, I didn't get your response.</Say>
  <Redirect>listener.php</Redirect>
</Response>
```

5. Update `input.php` as follows:

```php
<?php
  header('Content-type: text/xml');
  echo '<?xml version="1.0" encoding="UTF-8"?>';
  echo '<Response>';
  $user_pushed = (int) $_REQUEST['Digits'];
  switch( $user_pushed ){
    case 1:
      echo '<Say>Our store hours are 8 AM to 8 PM
        everyday.</Say>';
      break;
    case '2';
      echo '<Say>My pretend company is located at 101 4th
        Street in Neverland</Say>';
      echo '<Gather action="input.php" numDigits="1">';
      echo '<Say>For directions from the First Star to the
        right, press 6</Say>';
      echo '<Say>For directions from San Jose, press 7</Say>';
      echo '</Gather>';
      echo "<Say>Sorry, I didn't get your response.</Say>";
      echo '<Redirect method="GET">listener.php
        </Redirect>';
      break;
    case 3:
      echo '<Gather action="extensions.php"
        numDigits="1">';
      echo "<Say>Please enter your party's extension.
        </Say>";
      echo '<Say>Press 0 to return to the main menu</Say>';
      echo '</Gather>';
      echo "<Say>Sorry, I didn't get your response.</Say>";
```

```
    echo '<Redirect method="GET">input.php?Digits=2
      </Redirect>';
    break;
  case 4:
    echo '<Play>duck.mp3</Play>';
    break;
  case 5:
    echo '<Say>Please leave a message.</Say>';
    echo '<Redirect>voicemail.php</Redirect>';
    break;
  case 6:
    echo '<Say>Take the first star to the right
      and follow it straight on to the dawn.</Say>';
    break;
  case 7:
    echo '<Say>Take Cal Train to the Milbrae BART
      station. Take any Bart train to Powell Street
      </Say>';
    break;
  default:
    echo "<Say>Sorry, I can't do that yet.</Say>";
    echo '<Redirect>listener.php</Redirect>';
    break;
  }
  echo '<Pause/>';
  echo '<Say>Main Menu</Say>';
  echo '<Redirect>listener.php</Redirect>';
  echo '</Response>';
?>
```

6. Update `screen.php` as follows:

```
<?php
  header('Content-type: text/xml');
  echo '<?xml version="1.0" encoding="UTF-8"?>';
  echo '<Response>';
  $user_pushed = (int) $_REQUEST['Digits'];
  switch( $user_pushed ){
    case 1:
      echo '<Say>Connecting you to the caller. All calls
        are
        recorded.</Say>';
      break;
    default:
      echo '<Pause/>';
      echo '<Say>Main Menu</Say>';
```

```
            echo '<Redirect>listener.php</Redirect>';
            break;
      }
      echo '</Response>';
   ?>
```

7. Upload a new file called `voicemail.php` as follows:

```php
<?php
   include 'Services/Twilio.php';
   include("config.php");

   $myemail = 'MYEMAIL@me.com';
   $message = 'Pretend company is not available right now.
     Please leave a message.';
   $transcribe = true;

   $client = new Services_Twilio($accountsid, $authtoken);
   $response = new Services_Twilio_Twiml();

     //setup from email headers
   $headers = 'From: voicemail@mywebsite.com' . "\r\n"
     .'Reply-To: voicemail@mywebsite.com' . "\r\n" .'X-
     Mailer: Twilio Voicemail';

   // grab the to and from phone numbers
   $from = strlen($_REQUEST['From']) ? $_REQUEST['From'] :
     $_REQUEST['Caller'];
   $to = strlen($_REQUEST['To']) ? $_REQUEST['To'] :
     $_REQUEST['Called'];

   if( strtolower($_REQUEST['TranscriptionStatus']) ==
     "completed") {
     $body = "You have a new voicemail from " . ($from) .
       "\n\n";
     $body .= "Text of the transcribed voicemail:
       \n{$_REQUEST['TranscriptionText']}.\n\n";
     $body .= "Click this link to listen to the message:
       \n{$_REQUEST['RecordingUrl']}.mp3";
     mail($myemail, "New Voicemail Message from " . ($from),
       $body, $headers);
     die;
   } else if(strtolower($_REQUEST['TranscriptionStatus']) ==
     "failed") {
     $body = "You have a new voicemail from ".($from)."
       \n\n";
```

```
$body .= "Click this link to listen to the message:
    \n{$_REQUEST['RecordingUrl']}.mp3";
mail($myemail, "New Voicemail Message from " . ($from),
    $body, $headers);
die;
} else if(strlen($_REQUEST['RecordingUrl'])) {
$response->say("Thanks.  Good bye.");
$response->hangup();
if(strlen($transcribe) && strtolower($transcribe) !=
    'true') {
  $body = "You have a new voicemail from
    ".($from)."\n\n";
  $body .= "Click this link to listen to the message:
    \n{$_REQUEST['RecordingUrl']}.mp3";
  mail($myemail, "New Voicemail Message from " .
    ($from), $body, $headers);
}
} else {
$response->say( $message );
if( $transcribe )
  $params = array("transcribe"=>"true",
    "transcribeCallback"=>"{$_SERVER['SCRIPT_URI']}");
else
  $params = array();
$response->record($params);
}
$response->Respond();
?>
```

How it works...

We downloaded the Twilio PHP Library and uploaded it to our `Services` folder.

We've also updated `config.php`, `listener.php`, `screen.php`, and `input.php`.

Now, when the caller calls in, they'll get a list of options, including leaving a voicemail message.

Also, if a call to an agent doesn't go through, we're going to redirect that call back to the main menu instead of hanging up the call. This gives the caller the option to leave a new voicemail message for the company.

Sending an SMS to your Salesforce.com contacts

This last recipe is slightly different. Since we've been talking about IVRs and touching on CRMs, I thought you might find it interesting to make use of another popular CRM, www.Salesforce.com.

This system will grab the contacts out of our www.Salesforce.com account and send them each an SMS.

You will need a www.Salesforce.com account for this; you can get a free developer account at http://developer.force.com/.

Then you have to enter three credentials: your Salesforce username, your password, and your security token. You can find your security token by going to "setup" and clicking on **Reset Security Token**, as shown in the following screenshot:

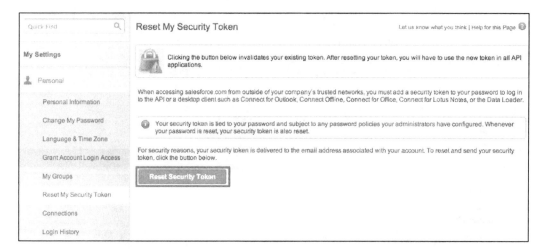

This will then be emailed to you as Salesforce doesn't actually keep your token. They store a hash of it in a similar way to how you would store passwords.

Getting Ready

The complete source code for this recipe can be found in the Chapter8/Recipe7 folder.

How to do it...

This app will use Salesforce's `www.force.com` API to send an SMS message to our contacts.

1. Download the `www.Salesforce.com` PHP toolkit from `http://wiki.developerforce.com/page/PHP_Toolkit_13.1` and upload the files into your `Services` folder.

2. Download the Twilio Helper Library from `https://github.com/twilio/twilio-php/zipball/master` and unzip it.

3. Upload the `Services/` folder on your website.

4. Upload `config.php` on your website and make sure the following variables are set:

```php
<?php

define("SF_USERNAME", "");
define("SF_PASSWORD", "");
define("SF_SECURITY_TOKEN", "");

$accountsid = '';//YOUR TWILIO ACCOUNT SID
$authtoken = '';//YOUR TWILIO AUTH TOKEN
$fromNumber = '';//PHONE NUMBER CALLS WILL COME FROM
```

5. Upload a file called `force.php` on your server:

```php
<?php
  session_start();
  include 'Services/Twilio.php';
  include("config.php");
  require_once ('Services/soapclient/SforceEnterpriseClient.php');

  $message = "{{name}} Try our new hot and ready pizza!";

  $client = new Services_Twilio($accountsid, $authtoken);

  $mySforceConnection = new SforceEnterpriseClient();
  $mySforceConnection->createConnection("Services/soapclient/
enterprise.wsdl.xml");
  $mySforceConnection->login(SF_USERNAME,
    SF_PASSWORD.SF_SECURITY_TOKEN);

  $query = "SELECT Id, FirstName, LastName, Phone from Contact";
  $response = $mySforceConnection->query($query);

  echo "Results of query '$query'<br/><br/>\n";
```

```php
foreach ($response->records as $record) {
  echo "Sending message to ".$record->FirstName . " " .
    $record->LastName . " at " . $record->Phone . "<br/>\n";
  $msg = str_replace("{{name}}",$record->FirstName,$message);
  $sid = send_sms($record->Phone, $msg);
}
exit;

function send_sms($number,$message){
  global $client,$fromNumber;
  $sms = $client->account->sms_messages->create(
    $fromNumber,
    $number,
    $message
  );
  return $sms->sid;
}
```

How it works...

In step 1, we downloaded the PHP toolkit from www.Salesforce.com; this toolkit lets us talk to the www.Salesforce.com API.

In steps 2 and 3, we downloaded and installed the Twilio Helper Library for PHP; this library is the heart of your Twilio-powered apps.

In step 4, we uploaded config.php that contains our authentication information to talk to the Salesforce and Twilio APIs.

Finally, in step 5, we uploaded our force.php file.

force.php will connect to Twilio and www.Salesforce.com and perform a query to get all of our contacts. It will then send each of them a personalized SMS message.

Building Your Own PBX

9

In this chapter we will cover the following:

- ▸ Getting started with PBX
- ▸ Setting up a subaccount for each user
- ▸ Letting a user purchase a custom phone number
- ▸ Allowing users to make calls from their call logs
- ▸ Allowing incoming phone calls
- ▸ Allowing outgoing phone calls
- ▸ Deleting a subaccount

Introduction

We're going to build a basic PBX system today that will let you have multiple users, each with their own phone number, and also give them the ability to handle calls.

This will serve as a basic Google Voice type system.

We're going to cover how to set up each user account with their own subaccount at Twilio and assign each subaccount with a phone number.

We're also going to set those phone numbers up to call the user's registered phone number, allowing the user to see a log of incoming calls and use "Click-to-Call" for those incoming phone numbers, and finally we're going to show you how to delete the user from your site.

We're also going to use a handy PHP micro framework called **Jolt** to build this application.

Getting started with PBX

First, let's set up our basic application.

As I previously mentioned, we're building this application using the Jolt micro framework, which is a mini MVC framework that I developed and used for many applications.

I'm going to go over a basic introduction to it so that you can see how it all works and then as we go through each recipe, we'll build on our application until we get a nice, handy system.

You can download the Jolt framework from `http://joltframework.com/`.

Jolt works in an interesting way; we set it up so that the `get` and `post` portions of the site are separated as shown in the following code snippet:

```php
<?php
include 'jolt.php';
$app = new Jolt('my app');
$app->get('/greet', function () use ($app){
    // render a view
    $app->render( 'page', array(
        "pageTitle"=>"Greetings",
        "body"=>"Greetings world!"
    ));
});
$app->post('/greet', function () use ($app){
    // render a view
    $app->render( 'page', array(
        "pageTitle"=>"Greetings",
        "body"=>"Greetings world!"
    ));
});
$app->get('/', function()  use ($app) {
    $app->render('home');
});
$app->listen();
?>
```

This will build a basic application that has an index and a greeting page. However, the greetings page shows both the `get ()` and `post ()` methods, which means that a loading/greeting with `get` (meaning, not called from a form) will result in one page, and a loading/greeting as a form submission will get you something entirely different. You can also add `route ()`, if you don't care about `get ()` or `post ()`, or add `put ()` and `delete ()`.

Another useful feature of Jolt is the session store; if we called the `$app->store("name","test");` method, we can call `$name = $app->store('name');` at any point in time and return the variable we assigned. This is useful for storing data that needs to be retrieved across the site, such as a logged-in user.

One thing you will notice is that instead of having multiple PHP files for each page, we created a new route.

Getting ready

The complete source code for this recipe can be found in the `Chapter9/Recipe1` folder in the source code for this book.

How to do it...

This recipe will download the necessary pieces and set it up for our PBX.

We're going to set up the application using the following steps:

1. Download the Jolt framework from `http://joltframework.com/`.

2. Create a folder called `system`.

3. Upload `jolt.php`, `functions.php`, and `pdo.class.php` to the `system` folder.

4. Upload the `.htaccess` file to your website.

```
RewriteEngine On
# RewriteBase /
RewriteCond %{REQUEST_FILENAME} !-f
RewriteCond %{REQUEST_FILENAME} !-d
RewriteRule ^ index.php [QSA,L]
```

 Jolt does require `mod_rewrite`, which is a standard on most server setups.

5. Create a folder called `views`.

6. Upload a file in `views` called `layout.php` with the following content:

```
<html>
<head>
  <title><?=$pageTitle?></title>
  <meta name="viewport" content="width=device-width, initial-scale=1.0">
  <link href="//netdna.bootstrapcdn.com/twitter-bootstrap/2.3.0/css/bootstrap-combined.no-icons.min.css" rel="stylesheet">
```

```
    <link href="//netdna.bootstrapcdn.com/font-awesome/3.0.2/css/
font-awesome.css" rel="stylesheet">
    <link href="//netdna.bootstrapcdn.com/font-awesome/3.0.2/css/
font-awesome-ie7.css" rel="stylesheet">
      <link href="//netdna.bootstrapcdn.com/twitter-bootstrap/2.3.0/
css/bootstrap-responsive.min.css" rel="stylesheet">
    <script src="//ajax.googleapis.com/ajax/libs/jquery/1.9.1/
jquery.min.js"></script>
    <script src="//netdna.bootstrapcdn.com/twitter-bootstrap/2.3.0/
js/bootstrap.min.js"></script>
</head>
<body>
  <div class="container">
    <div class="masthead">
      <h3 class="muted">My PBX</h3>
      <div class="navbar">
        <div class="navbar-inner">
          <div class="container">
            <ul class="nav">
              <li class="active"><a href="<?=$uri?>/">Home</a></
li>
              <li><a href="<?=$uri?>/login">Login</a></li>
              <li><a href="<?=$uri?>/signup">Signup</a></li>
            </ul>
          </div>
        </div>
      </div><!-- /.navbar -->
    </div>
    <?=$pageContent?>
    <hr />
    <div class="footer">
      <p>&copy; MY PBX <?=date("Y")?></p>
    </div>
  </div> <!-- /container -->
</body>
</html>
```

7. Download the Twilio Helper Library from `https://github.com/twilio/twilio-php/zipball/master` and unzip the file.

8. Upload the `Services/` folder to your website.

9. Add `sql.sql` to your database.

10. Upload `config.ini` to the site that contains the following content:

```ini
;site settings
site.name = my site
site.url =

; rendering vars
views.root = views
views.layout = layout

; session vars
cookies.secret = IeNj0yt0sQu33zeflUFfym0nk1e
cookies.flash = _F

;  twilio vars
twilio.accountsid =
twilio.authtoken =
twilio.fromNumber =
;  database vars
mysql.dbhost =
mysql.dbname =
mysql.dbuser =
mysql.dbpass =
```

> You may notice this file is laid out slightly differently than your previous `config.php` files because of the way this framework works. Instead of separate variables, we store them in an `.ini` file that is read by the Jolt system store. Then, instead of calling `$dbhost`, we will call `$app->option('mysql.dbhost')`.

11. Upload `index.php` (containing the following content) to your site as follows:

```php
<?php
include 'Services/Twilio.php';
require("config.php");
require("system/jolt.php");
require("system/pdo.class.php");
require("system/functions.php");

$_GET['route'] = isset($_GET['route']) ? '/'.$_GET['route'] : '/';
$app = new Jolt('site',false);
$app->option('source', 'config.ini');
$mysiteURL = $app->option('site.url');

$app->get('/', function() use ($app){
```

```
    $app->render( 'home' );
});
$app->listen();
```

12. Upload the following `home.php` file to your `views` folder:

```html
<div class="jumbotron">
  <h1>My PBX</h1>
  <p class="lead">
    This is a basic PBX system built for the Twilio Cookbook
  </p>
</div>
```

How it works...

In steps 1, 2, 3, 4, and 5, we downloaded and installed the Jolt framework for PHP. We also set up a `system` and `views` folder.

In step 6, we created `layout.php`, which is our layout for the site.

In steps 7 and 8, we downloaded and installed the Twilio Helper Library for PHP. This library is the heart of your Twilio-powered apps.

In step 9, we loaded our database schema into our database.

In step 10, we set up our `config.ini` file.

In step 11, we set up our barebones `index.php` file, which doesn't do much right now.

Finally, in step 12, we set up `home.php`, which is the first page people will see when they load the site in their browser.

When you load the app now, you'll go to the `index` file, which is specified by `$app->get("/")` route.

All this page does is load the `home.php` file found in the `views` folder.

We've set up the basic framework for our PBX system. Now let's make it actually do something.

Setting up a subaccount for each user

Before we can do anything else, we have to allow users to sign up.

To do this, we're going to build a joining form for users to join your PBX system. This form will also create their subaccount under your main Twilio account. Subaccounts make it easier to track a user's usage.

Getting ready

The complete source code for this recipe can be found in the `Chapter9/Recipe2` folder in the source code for this book.

How to do it...

Now that we've set up our basic framework, let's build a form to allow users to sign up and have Twilio create subaccounts for them.

1. Upload the following `index.php` file to your website:

```php
<?php
include 'Services/Twilio.php';
require("config.php");
require("system/jolt.php");
require("system/pdo.class.php");
require("system/functions.php");

$_GET['route'] = isset($_GET['route']) ? '/'.$_GET['route'] : '/';
$app = new Jolt('site',false);
$app->option('source', 'config.ini');
#$pdo = Db::singleton();
$mysiteURL = $app->option('site.url');

$app->get('/signup', function() use ($app){
        $app->render( 'register', array(),'layout' );
});
$app->post('/signup', function() use ($app){
  $client = new Services_Twilio($app->store('twilio.accountsid'),
$app->store('twilio.authtoken') );
  extract($_POST);
  $timestamp = strtotime( $timestamp );
  $subaccount = $client->accounts->create(array(
    "FriendlyName" => $email
  ));
  $sid = $subaccount->sid;
  $token = $subaccount->auth_token;
  $sql = "INSERT INTO 'user' SET `name`='{$name}',`email`='{$email
}',`password`='{$password}',`phone_number`='{$phone_number}',`sid`
='{$sid}',`token`='{$token}',`status`=1";
  $pdo = Db::singleton();
  $pdo->exec($sql);
  $uid = $pdo->lastInsertId();
  $app->store('user',$uid);
```

```
$app->redirect( $app->getBaseUri().'/phone-number');
});
$app->get('/', function() use ($app){
  $app->render( 'home' );
});
$app->listen();
```

2. Upload the following `register.php` file in your `views` folder:

```
<h2>Sign up</h2>
<form class="form-horizontal" action="<?=$uri?>/signup"
method="POST">
<table>
<tr>
  <td>Your Name</td>
  <td><input type="text" name="name" /></td>
</tr>
<tr>
  <td>Your Email</td>
  <td><input type="text" name="email" /></td>
</tr>
<tr>
  <td>Your Password</td>
  <td><input type="text" name="password" /></td>
</tr>
<tr>
  <td>Your Phone Number</td>
  <td><input type="text" name="phone_number" /></td>
</tr>
</table>
<button type="submit">Sign up</button>
</form>
```

How it works...

In step 1, we updated `index.php` to include the logic for the sign-up page.

In step 2, we uploaded `register.php`, which is a new view.

Now, when a user signs up, we will send his/her e-mail address to Twilio to create a subaccount. Then, Twilio will store his/her information in the database.

Letting a user purchase a custom phone number

Ok, once a user has signed up, he/she is going to need a phone number that he/she can call his/her own.

On signup, we forward the user to the /phone-number object, which is what we'll build in this recipe.

Getting ready

The complete source code for this recipe can be found in the Chapter9/Recipe3 folder in the source code for this book.

How to do it...

Our app will walk users through the process of searching for and purchasing a phone number using the following steps:

1. Update the following index.php file:

```php
<?php
include 'Services/Twilio.php';
require("config.php");
require("system/jolt.php");
require("system/pdo.class.php");
require("system/functions.php");

$_GET['route'] = isset($_GET['route']) ? '/'.$_GET['route'] : '/';
$app = new Jolt('site',false);
$app->option('source', 'config.ini');
#$pdo = Db::singleton();
$mysiteURL = $app->option('site.url');

$app->condition('signed_in', function () use ($app) {
        $app->redirect( $app->getBaseUri().'/login',!$app-
>store('user'));
});

$app->get('/login', function() use ($app){
        $app->render( 'login', array(),'layout' );
});
$app->post('/login', function() use ($app){
```

```php
    $sql = "SELECT * FROM `user` WHERE `email`='{$_POST['user']}'
AND `password`='{$_POST['pass']}'";
    $pdo = Db::singleton();
    $res = $pdo->query( $sql );
    $user = $res->fetch();
    if( isset($user['ID']) ){
      $app->store('user',$user['ID']);
            $app->redirect( $app->getBaseUri().'/home');
        }else{
            $app->redirect( $app->getBaseUri().'/login');
        }
});
$app->get('/signup', function() use ($app){
        $app->render( 'register', array(),'layout' );
});
$app->post('/signup', function() use ($app){
    $client = new Services_Twilio($app->store('twilio.accountsid'),
$app->store('twilio.authtoken') );
    extract($_POST);
    $timestamp = strtotime( $timestamp );
    $subaccount = $client->accounts->create(array(
      "FriendlyName" => $email
    ));
    $sid = $subaccount->sid;
    $token = $subaccount->auth_token;
    $sql = "INSERT INTO 'user' SET `name`='{$name}', `email`='{$email
}', `password`='{$password}', `phone_number`='{$phone_number}', `sid`
='{$sid}', `token`='{$token}', `status`=1";
    $pdo = Db::singleton();
    $pdo->exec($sql);
    $uid = $pdo->lastInsertId();
    $app->store('user',$uid );
    // log user in
      $app->redirect( $app->getBaseUri().'/phone-number');
});
$app->get('/phone-number', function() use ($app){
    $app->condition('signed_in');
    $user = $app->store('user');
    $client = new Services_Twilio($user['sid'], $user['token']);
    $app->render('phone-number');
});

$app->post("search", function() use ($app){
    $app->condition('signed_in');
    $user = get_user( $app->store('user') );
```

```
$client = new Services_Twilio($user['sid'], $user['token']);
$SearchParams = array();
$SearchParams['InPostalCode'] = !empty($_POST['postal_code']) ?
trim($_POST['postal_code']) : '';
$SearchParams['NearNumber'] = !empty($_POST['near_number']) ?
trim($_POST['near_number']) : '';
$SearchParams['Contains'] = !empty($_POST['contains'])? trim($_
POST['contains']) : '' ;
  try {
    $numbers = $client->account->available_phone_numbers-
>getList('US', 'Local', $SearchParams);
    if(empty($numbers)) {
      $err = urlencode("We didn't find any phone numbers by that
search");
      $app->redirect( $app->getBaseUri().'/phone-
number?msg='.$err);
      exit(0);
    }
  } catch (Exception $e) {
    $err = urlencode("Error processing search:
{$e->getMessage()}");
    $app->redirect( $app->getBaseUri().'/phone-number?msg='.$err);
    exit(0);
  }
  $app->render('search',array('numbers'=>$numbers));
});

$app->post("buy", function() use ($app){
  $app->condition('signed_in');
  $user = get_user( $app->store('user') );
  $client = new Services_Twilio($user['sid'], $user['token']);
  $PhoneNumber = $_POST['PhoneNumber'];
  try {
    $number = $client->account->incoming_phone_numbers-
>create(array(
      'PhoneNumber' => $PhoneNumber
    ));
    $phsid = $number->sid;
    if ( !empty($phsid) ){
      $sql = "INSERT INTO numbers (user_id,number,sid) VALUES('{$u
ser['ID']}','{$PhoneNumber}','{$phsid}');";
      $pdo = Db::singleton();
      $pdo->exec($sql);
      $fid = $pdo->lastInsertId();
      $ret = editNumber($phsid,array(
```

```
            "FriendlyName"=>$PhoneNumber,
            "VoiceUrl" => $mysiteURL."/voice?id=".$fid,
            "VoiceMethod" => "POST",
          ),$user['sid'], $user['token']);
        }
    } catch (Exception $e) {
        $err = urlencode("Error purchasing number:
{$e->getMessage()}");
        $app->redirect( $app->getBaseUri().'/phone-number?msg='.$err);
        exit(0);
    }
    $msg = urlencode("Thank you for purchasing $PhoneNumber");
    header("Location: index.php?msg=$msg");
    $app->redirect( $app->getBaseUri().'/home?msg='.$msg);
    exit(0);
});
$app->route('/voice', function() use ($app){

});
$app->get('/transcribe', function() use ($app){

});
$app->get('/logout', function() use ($app){
        $app->store('user',0);
        $app->redirect( $app->getBaseUri().'/login');
});
$app->get('/home', function() use ($app){
  $app->condition('signed_in');

});
$app->get('/', function() use ($app){
  $app->render( 'home' );
});
$app->listen();
```

2. Create a file called `phone-number.php` in your `views` folder with the following content:

```
<h3>Find a number to buy</h3>
<?php if(!empty($_GET['msg'])): ?>
  <p class="msg"><?php echo htmlspecialchars($_GET['msg']); ?></p>
<?php endif;?>
<form method="POST" action="<?=$uri?>/search">
<label>near US postal code (e.g. 94117): </label><input
type="text" size="4" name="postal_code"/><br/>
```

```html
<label>near this other number (e.g. +14156562345): </label><input
type="text" size="7" name="near_number"/><br/>
<label>matching this pattern (e.g. 415***EPIC): </label><input
type="text" size="7" name="contains"/><br/>
<input type="hidden" name="action" value="search" />
<input type="submit" name="submit" value="SEARCH"/>
</form>
```

3. Create a file called `search.php` in your `views` folder with the following content:

```php
<h3>Choose a Twilio number to buy</h3>
<?php   foreach($numbers->available_phone_numbers as $number){ ?>
  <form method="POST" action="<?=$uri?>/buy">
  <label><?php echo $number->friendly_name ?></label>
  <input type="hidden" name="PhoneNumber" value="<?php echo
$number->phone_number ?>">
    <input type="hidden" name="action" value="buy" />
    <input type="submit" name="submit" value="BUY" />
  </form>
<?php   }   ?>
```

How it works...

In step 1, we updated our `index.php` file to include the ability to purchase phone numbers.

When the user first comes to the page, we check to make sure he/she is logged in; if he/she is, we initialize the Twilio class using their credentials; otherwise, we present a form to log in.

Then we let them search for a phone number that they are interested in assigning to their account. Once they find a phone number and assign it to themselves, we insert the number in our database and instruct Twilio to forward all calls to `/voice`.

We'll touch on what `/voice` does shortly.

You may have also noticed that we set a condition:

```php
$app->condition('signed_in', function () use ($app) {
        $app->redirect( $app->getBaseUri().'/login',!$app-
>store('user'));
});
```

What this means is that whenever we call the `$app->condition('signed_in');` condition, and it fails, then we can redirect the user to the login page.

This comes in handy for setting up sections that require a user to be logged in; we simply add the `$app->condition('signed_in');` line, and if a person is not logged in, they get redirected to the login page.

Allowing users to make calls from their call logs

We're going to give your user a place to view their call log.

We will display a list of incoming calls and give them the option to call back on these numbers.

Getting ready

The complete source code for this recipe can be found in the `Chapter9/Recipe4` folder in the source code for this book.

How to do it...

Now, let's build a section for our users to log in to using the following steps:

1. Update a file called `index.php` with the following content:

```php
<?php
session_start();
include 'Services/Twilio.php';
require("system/jolt.php");
require("system/pdo.class.php");
require("system/functions.php");

$_GET['route'] = isset($_GET['route']) ? '/'.$_GET['route'] : '/';
$app = new Jolt('site',false);
$app->option('source', 'config.ini');
#$pdo = Db::singleton();
$mysiteURL = $app->option('site.url');

$app->condition('signed_in', function () use ($app) {
        $app->redirect( $app->getBaseUri().'/login',!$app-
>store('user'));
});

$app->get('/login', function() use ($app){
        $app->render( 'login', array(),'layout' );
});
$app->post('/login', function() use ($app){
  $sql = "SELECT * FROM `user` WHERE `email`='{$_POST['user']}'
AND `password`='{$_POST['pass']}'";
  $pdo = Db::singleton();
```

```
    $res = $pdo->query( $sql );
    $user = $res->fetch();
    if( isset($user['ID']) ){
      $_SESSION['uid'] = $user['ID'];
      $app->store('user',$user['ID']);
          $app->redirect( $app->getBaseUri().'/home');
      }else{
          $app->redirect( $app->getBaseUri().'/login');
      }
});
$app->get('/signup', function() use ($app){
        $app->render( 'register', array(),'layout' );
});
$app->post('/signup', function() use ($app){
  $client = new Services_Twilio($app->store('twilio.accountsid'),
$app->store('twilio.authtoken') );
  extract($_POST);
  $timestamp = strtotime( $timestamp );
  $subaccount = $client->accounts->create(array(
    "FriendlyName" => $email
  ));
  $sid = $subaccount->sid;
  $token = $subaccount->auth_token;
  $sql = "INSERT INTO 'user' SET `name`='{$name}', `email`='{$email
}', `password`='{$password}', `phone_number`='{$phone_number}', `sid`
='{$sid}', `token`='{$token}', `status`=1";
  $pdo = Db::singleton();
  $pdo->exec($sql);
  $uid = $pdo->lastInsertId();
  $app->store('user',$uid );
  // log user in
    $app->redirect( $app->getBaseUri().'/phone-number');
});
$app->get('/phone-number', function() use ($app){
  $app->condition('signed_in');
  $user = $app->store('user');
  $client = new Services_Twilio($user['sid'], $user['token']);
  $app->render('phone-number');
});

$app->post("search", function() use ($app){
  $app->condition('signed_in');
  $user = get_user( $app->store('user') );
```

```
  $client = new Services_Twilio($user['sid'], $user['token']);
  $SearchParams = array();
  $SearchParams['InPostalCode'] = !empty($_POST['postal_code']) ?
trim($_POST['postal_code']) : '';
  $SearchParams['NearNumber'] = !empty($_POST['near_number']) ?
trim($_POST['near_number']) : '';
  $SearchParams['Contains'] = !empty($_POST['contains'])? trim($_
POST['contains']) : '' ;
   try {
     $numbers = $client->account->available_phone_numbers-
>getList('US', 'Local', $SearchParams);
      if(empty($numbers)) {
       $err = urlencode("We didn't find any phone numbers by that
search");
       $app->redirect( $app->getBaseUri().'/phone-
number?msg='.$err);
        exit(0);
      }
   } catch (Exception $e) {
     $err = urlencode("Error processing search:
{$e->getMessage()}");
     $app->redirect( $app->getBaseUri().'/phone-number?msg='.$err);
     exit(0);
   }
   $app->render('search',array('numbers'=>$numbers));
});


$app->post("buy", function() use ($app){
  $app->condition('signed_in');
  $user = get_user( $app->store('user') );
  $client = new Services_Twilio($user['sid'], $user['token']);
  $PhoneNumber = $_POST['PhoneNumber'];
   try {
     $number = $client->account->incoming_phone_numbers-
>create(array(
       'PhoneNumber' => $PhoneNumber
     ));
     $phsid = $number->sid;
     if ( !empty($phsid) ){
       $sql = "INSERT INTO numbers (user_id,number,sid) VALUES('{$u
ser['ID']}','{$PhoneNumber}','{$phsid}');";
       $pdo = Db::singleton();
       $pdo->exec($sql);
```

```php
        $fid = $pdo->lastInsertId();
        $ret = editNumber($phsid,array(
          "FriendlyName"=>$PhoneNumber,
          "VoiceUrl" => $mysiteURL."/voice?id=".$fid,
          "VoiceMethod" => "POST",
        ),$user['sid'], $user['token']);
    }
  } catch (Exception $e) {
    $err = urlencode("Error purchasing number:
{$e->getMessage()}");
    $app->redirect( $app->getBaseUri().'/phone-number?msg='.$err);
    exit(0);
  }
  $msg = urlencode("Thank you for purchasing $PhoneNumber");
  header("Location: index.php?msg=$msg");
  $app->redirect( $app->getBaseUri().'/home?msg='.$msg);
  exit(0);
});
$app->route('/voice', function() use ($app){
});
$app->get('/transcribe', function() use ($app){
});
$app->get('/logout', function() use ($app){
        $app->store('user',0);
        $app->redirect( $app->getBaseUri().'/login');
});
$app->get('/home', function() use ($app){
  $app->condition('signed_in');
  $uid = $app->store('user');
  $user = get_user( $uid );
  $client = new Services_Twilio($user['sid'], $user['token']);
  $app->render('dashboard',array(
    'user'=>$user,
    'client'=>$client
  ));
});
$app->get('/delete', function() use ($app){
  $app->condition('signed_in');
});
$app->get('/', function() use ($app){
  $app->render( 'home' );
});
$app->listen();
```

2. Upload a file called `dashboard.php` with the following content to your `views` folder:

```php
<h2>My Number</h2>
<?php
  $pdo = Db::singleton();
  $sql = "SELECT * FROM `numbers` WHERE `user_
id`='{$user['ID']}'";
  $res = $pdo->query( $sql );
  while( $row = $res->fetch() ){
    echo preg_replace("/[^0-9]/", "", $row['number']);
  }
  try {
?>
    <h2>My Call History</h2>
    <p>Here are a list of recent calls, you can click any number
to call them back, we will call your registered phone number and
then the caller</p>
    <table width=100% class="table table-hover tabled-striped">
    <thead>
    <tr>
      <th>From</th>
      <th>To</th>
      <th>Start Date</th>
      <th>End Date</th>
      <th>Duration</th>
    </tr>
    </thead>
    <tbody>
<?php
    foreach ($client->account->calls as $call) {
#      echo "<p>Call from $call->from to $call->to at $call-
>start_time of length $call->duration</p>";
      if( !stristr($call->direction,'inbound') )
    continue;
      $type = find_in_list($call->from);
?>
    <tr>
      <td><a href="<?=$uri?>/call?number=<?=urlencode($call-
>from)?>"><?=$call->from?></a></td>
      <td><?=$call->to?></td>
      <td><?=$call->start_time?></td>
      <td><?=$call->end_time?></td>
      <td><?=$call->duration?></td>
    </tr>
<?php
```

```
    }
?>
    </tbody>
    </table>
<?php
    } catch (Exception $e) {
        echo 'Error: ' . $e->getMessage();
    }
?>
    <hr />
    <a href="<?=$uri?>/delete" onclick="return confirm('Are you sure
you wish to close your account?');">Delete My Account</a>
```

How it works...

In step 1, we updated the index.php file.

In step 2, we uploaded dashboard.php to the views folder. This file checks if we're logged in using the $app->condition('signed_in') method, which we discussed earlier, and if we are, it displays all incoming calls we've had to our account. We can then push a button to call one of those numbers and whitelist or blacklist them.

We also give the user the option to delete the account, which we'll cover in the *Deleting a subaccount* recipe.

Allowing incoming phone calls

Part of the whole reason for setting up this system is to allow incoming calls.

This recipe will take an incoming call to the phone number your user has assigned to his/her account and forward it to the phone number he/she registered with on the joining page.

If the user is away and can't answer the phone at that time, the system will ask the caller to leave a message and e-mail the voicemail to the user.

We're also going to compare the number against our white and blacklists, which we created in the previous recipe, and if the person is blacklisted, or if the call is after 5 p.m. and the number is not whitelisted, we'll direct them straight to voicemail.

Getting ready

The complete source code for this recipe can be found in the Chapter9/Recipe5 folder in the source code for this book.

How to do it...

How do we handle calls to our users' purchased phone numbers? This recipe will show you how to make the `/voice` page actually do something handy.

Update `index.php` with the following content:

```php
<?php
session_start();
include 'Services/Twilio.php';
require("system/jolt.php");
require("system/pdo.class.php");
require("system/functions.php");

$_GET['route'] = isset($_GET['route']) ? '/'.$_GET['route'] : '/';
$app = new Jolt('site',false);
$app->option('source', 'config.ini');
#$pdo = Db::singleton();
$mysiteURL = $app->option('site.url');

$app->condition('signed_in', function () use ($app) {
        $app->redirect( $app->getBaseUri().'/login',!$app-
>store('user'));
});

$app->get('/login', function() use ($app){
        $app->render( 'login', array(),'layout' );
});
$app->post('/login', function() use ($app){
  $sql = "SELECT * FROM `user` WHERE `email`='{$_POST['user']}' AND
`password`='{$_POST['pass']}'";
  $pdo = Db::singleton();
  $res = $pdo->query( $sql );
  $user = $res->fetch();
  if( isset($user['ID']) ){
    $_SESSION['uid'] = $user['ID'];
    $app->store('user',$user['ID']);
        $app->redirect( $app->getBaseUri().'/home');
    }else{
        $app->redirect( $app->getBaseUri().'/login');
    }
});
$app->get('/signup', function() use ($app){
        $app->render( 'register', array(),'layout' );
});
```

```php
$app->post('/signup', function() use ($app){
  $client = new Services_Twilio($app->store('twilio.accountsid'),
$app->store('twilio.authtoken') );
  extract($_POST);
  $timestamp = strtotime( $timestamp );
  $subaccount = $client->accounts->create(array(
    "FriendlyName" => $email
  ));
  $sid = $subaccount->sid;
  $token = $subaccount->auth_token;
  $sql = "INSERT INTO 'user' SET `name`='{$name}',`email`='{$email}',`
password`='{$password}',`phone_number`='{$phone_number}',`sid`='{$sid}
',`token`='{$token}',`status`=1";
  $pdo = Db::singleton();
  $pdo->exec($sql);
  $uid = $pdo->lastInsertId();
  $app->store('user',$uid );
  // log user in
    $app->redirect( $app->getBaseUri().'/phone-number');
});
$app->get('/phone-number', function() use ($app){
  $app->condition('signed_in');
  $user = $app->store('user');
  $client = new Services_Twilio($user['sid'], $user['token']);
  $app->render('phone-number');
});
$app->post("search", function() use ($app){
  $app->condition('signed_in');
  $user = get_user( $app->store('user') );
  $client = new Services_Twilio($user['sid'], $user['token']);
  $SearchParams = array();
  $SearchParams['InPostalCode'] = !empty($_POST['postal_code']) ?
trim($_POST['postal_code']) : '';
  $SearchParams['NearNumber'] = !empty($_POST['near_number']) ?
trim($_POST['near_number']) : '';
  $SearchParams['Contains'] = !empty($_POST['contains'])? trim($_
POST['contains']) : '' ;
  try {
    $numbers = $client->account->available_phone_numbers-
>getList('US', 'Local', $SearchParams);
    if(empty($numbers)) {
      $err = urlencode("We didn't find any phone numbers by that
search");
      $app->redirect( $app->getBaseUri().'/phone-number?msg='.$err);
      exit(0);
```

```php
      }
    } catch (Exception $e) {
      $err = urlencode("Error processing search: {$e->getMessage()}");
      $app->redirect( $app->getBaseUri().'/phone-number?msg='.$err);
      exit(0);
    }
    $app->render('search',array('numbers'=>$numbers));
});
$app->post("buy", function() use ($app){
  $app->condition('signed_in');
  $user = get_user( $app->store('user') );
  $client = new Services_Twilio($user['sid'], $user['token']);
  $PhoneNumber = $_POST['PhoneNumber'];
  try {
    $number = $client->account->incoming_phone_numbers->create(array(
      'PhoneNumber' => $PhoneNumber
    ));
    $phsid = $number->sid;
    if ( !empty($phsid) ){
      $sql = "INSERT INTO numbers (user_id,number,sid) VALUES ('{$user[
'ID']}','{$PhoneNumber}','{$phsid}');";
      $pdo = Db::singleton();
      $pdo->exec($sql);
      $fid = $pdo->lastInsertId();
      $ret = editNumber($phsid,array(
        "FriendlyName"=>$PhoneNumber,
        "VoiceUrl" => $mysiteURL."/voice?id=".$fid,
        "VoiceMethod" => "POST",
      ),$user['sid'], $user['token']);
    }
  } catch (Exception $e) {
    $err = urlencode("Error purchasing number: {$e->getMessage()}");
    $app->redirect( $app->getBaseUri().'/phone-number?msg='.$err);
    exit(0);
  }
  $msg = urlencode("Thank you for purchasing $PhoneNumber");
  header("Location: index.php?msg=$msg");
  $app->redirect( $app->getBaseUri().'/home?msg='.$msg);
  exit(0);
});
$app->route('/voice', function() use ($app){
  header("Content-type: text/xml");
  $fid = $_GET['id'];
  $from = preg_replace("/[^0-9]/", "", $_POST['From']);
```

```php
    $pdo = Db::singleton();
    $sql = "SELECT * FROM numbers WHERE ID='{$fid}';";
    $res = $pdo->query( $sql );
    $number = $res->fetch();
    $fromNumber = $number['number'];
    if( $user = get_user($number['user_id']) ){
      $_SESSION['uid'] = $user['ID'];
      $toNumber = $user['phone_number'];
      $name = $user['name'];
      $response = new Services_Twilio_Twiml();
      $response->dial($toNumber, array('timeout' => 5));
      $response->say("I'm sorry, $name is not available at this time.
Please leave a message after the tone.");
      $response->record(array(
        'transcribeCallback' => 'transcribe.
php?uid='.$user['ID'].'&From=' . $from,
        'transcribe' => 'true'
      ));
      print $response;
      exit;
    }


});
$app-> route('/transcribe', function() use ($app){
  header("Content-type: text/xml");
  $uid = $_GET['uid'];
  if( $user = get_user( $uid ) ){
    $filter      = "!@#$^&%*()+=-[]\/{}|:<>?,.";
    $recording  = preg_replace("/[$filter]/", "", $_
POST['RecordingUrl']);
    $transcript = preg_replace("/[$filter]/", "", $_
POST['TranscriptionText']);
    $from    = preg_replace("/[^0-9]/", "", $_GET['From']);
    $subject = "You have a new voicemail transcription from " . $from;
    $body = "You received voicemail." .
              "\n\nHere is the recording: $recording" .
              "\n\nAnd here is the transcription:\n $transcript";
    mail($user['email'], $subject, $body);
    exit;
  }
});

$app->get('/logout', function() use ($app){
        $app->store('user',0);
        $app->redirect( $app->getBaseUri().'/login');
```

```
  });
  $app->get('/home', function() use ($app){
    $app->condition('signed_in');
    $uid = $app->store('user');
    $user = get_user( $uid );
    $client = new Services_Twilio($user['sid'], $user['token']);
    $app->render('dashboard',array(
      'user'=>$user,
      'client'=>$client
    ));
  });
  $app->get('/delete', function() use ($app){
    $app->condition('signed_in');
  });
  $app->get('/', function() use ($app){
    $app->render( 'home' );
  });
  $app->listen();
```

How it works...

We've just added the /voice and /transcribe pages to our web app.

Now, whenever the user receives an incoming call on the number assigned to his/her account, it will automatically forward the call to the registered phone number.

If the call times out, we prompt the caller to leave a message. This message then triggers /transcribe that takes the recordings and e-mails it to the user, along with a transcription.

On top of this, we've also added a check to see if the caller is whitelisted, blacklisted, or calling during office hours.

If the call is between 9 a.m. and 5 p.m. and the caller is neither whitelisted nor blacklisted, the call goes through. If the call is between 5 p.m. and 9 a.m. and the caller is not whitelisted, the call goes straight to voicemail, and if the caller is blacklisted, he/she gets sent straight to voicemail regardless of the other conditions met.

Allowing outgoing phone calls

We've given users the ability to handle incoming calls. Now let's give them the ability to call people back from their account.

In index.php, we displayed a link on each phone number that lets the user use the "Click-to-Call" feature. Now, let's build up on this recipe.

Getting ready

The complete source code for this recipe can be found in the `Chapter9/Recipe6` folder in the source code for this book.

How to do it...

Once we're finished, we'll be able to click any phone number and make an outgoing call. This call will first call us and then the phone number we clicked on. Perform the following step to do so.

Update `index.php` again with our new routes as follows:

```php
<?php
session_start();
include 'Services/Twilio.php';
require("system/jolt.php");
require("system/pdo.class.php");
require("system/functions.php");

$_GET['route'] = isset($_GET['route']) ? '/'.$_GET['route'] : '/';
$app = new Jolt('site',false);
$app->option('source', 'config.ini');
#$pdo = Db::singleton();
$mysiteURL = $app->option('site.url');

$app->condition('signed_in', function () use ($app) {
        $app->redirect( $app->getBaseUri().'/login',!$app-
>store('user'));
});

$app->get('/login', function() use ($app){
        $app->render( 'login', array(),'layout' );
});
$app->post('/login', function() use ($app){
  $sql = "SELECT * FROM `user` WHERE `email`='{$_POST['user']}' AND
`password`='{$_POST['pass']}'";
  $pdo = Db::singleton();
  $res = $pdo->query( $sql );
  $user = $res->fetch();
  if( isset($user['ID']) ){
    $_SESSION['uid'] = $user['ID'];
    $app->store('user',$user['ID']);
        $app->redirect( $app->getBaseUri().'/home');
```

```
    }else{
        $app->redirect( $app->getBaseUri().'/login');
    }
});
$app->get('/signup', function() use ($app){
        $app->render( 'register', array(),'layout' );
});
$app->post('/signup', function() use ($app){
  $client = new Services_Twilio($app->store('twilio.accountsid'),
$app->store('twilio.authtoken') );
  extract($_POST);
  $timestamp = strtotime( $timestamp );
  $subaccount = $client->accounts->create(array(
    "FriendlyName" => $email
  ));
  $sid = $subaccount->sid;
  $token = $subaccount->auth_token;
  $sql = "INSERT INTO 'user' SET `name`='{$name}',`email`='{$email}',`
password`='{$password}',`phone_number`='{$phone_number}',`sid`='{$sid}
',`token`='{$token}',`status`=1";
  $pdo = Db::singleton();
  $pdo->exec($sql);
  $uid = $pdo->lastInsertId();
  $app->store('user',$uid );
  //  log user in
    $app->redirect( $app->getBaseUri().'/phone-number');
});
$app->get('/phone-number', function() use ($app){
  $app->condition('signed_in');
  $user = $app->store('user');
  $client = new Services_Twilio($user['sid'], $user['token']);
  $app->render('phone-number');
});

$app->post("search", function() use ($app){
  $app->condition('signed_in');
  $user = get_user( $app->store('user') );
  $client = new Services_Twilio($user['sid'], $user['token']);
  $SearchParams = array();
  $SearchParams['InPostalCode'] = !empty($_POST['postal_code']) ?
trim($_POST['postal_code']) : '';
  $SearchParams['NearNumber'] = !empty($_POST['near_number']) ?
trim($_POST['near_number']) : '';
  $SearchParams['Contains'] = !empty($_POST['contains'])? trim($_
POST['contains']) : '' ;
```

```
  try {
    $numbers = $client->account->available_phone_numbers-
>getList('US', 'Local', $SearchParams);
    if(empty($numbers)) {
      $err = urlencode("We didn't find any phone numbers by that
search");
      $app->redirect( $app->getBaseUri().'/phone-number?msg='.$err);
      exit(0);
    }
  } catch (Exception $e) {
    $err = urlencode("Error processing search: {$e->getMessage()}");
    $app->redirect( $app->getBaseUri().'/phone-number?msg='.$err);
    exit(0);
  }
  $app->render('search',array('numbers'=>$numbers));
});

$app->post("buy", function() use ($app){
  $app->condition('signed_in');
  $user = get_user( $app->store('user') );
  $client = new Services_Twilio($user['sid'], $user['token']);
  $PhoneNumber = $_POST['PhoneNumber'];
  try {
    $number = $client->account->incoming_phone_numbers->create(array(
      'PhoneNumber' => $PhoneNumber
    ));
    $phsid = $number->sid;
    if ( !empty($phsid) ){
      $sql = "INSERT INTO numbers (user_id,number,sid) VALUES('{$user[
'ID']}','{$PhoneNumber}','{$phsid}');";
      $pdo = Db::singleton();
      $pdo->exec($sql);
      $fid = $pdo->lastInsertId();
      $ret = editNumber($phsid,array(
        "FriendlyName"=>$PhoneNumber,
        "VoiceUrl" => $mysiteURL."/voice?id=".$fid,
        "VoiceMethod" => "POST",
      ),$user['sid'], $user['token']);
    }
  } catch (Exception $e) {
    $err = urlencode("Error purchasing number: {$e->getMessage()}");
    $app->redirect( $app->getBaseUri().'/phone-number?msg='.$err);
    exit(0);
  }
```

```php
    $msg = urlencode("Thank you for purchasing $PhoneNumber");
    header("Location: index.php?msg=$msg");
    $app->redirect( $app->getBaseUri().'/home?msg='.$msg);
    exit(0);
});
$app->route('/voice', function() use ($app){
    header("Content-type: text/xml");
    $fid = $_GET['id'];
    $from = preg_replace("/[^0-9]/", "", $_POST['From']);
    $pdo = Db::singleton();
    $sql = "SELECT * FROM numbers WHERE ID='{$fid}';";
    $res = $pdo->query( $sql );
    $number = $res->fetch();
    $fromNumber = $number['number'];
    if( $user = get_user($number['user_id']) ){
        $_SESSION['uid'] = $user['ID'];
        $toNumber = $user['phone_number'];
        $name = $user['name'];
        $response = new Services_Twilio_Twiml();
        $response->dial($toNumber, array('timeout' => 5));
        $response->say("I'm sorry, $name is not available at this time.
Please leave a message after the tone.");
        $response->record(array(
            'transcribeCallback' => 'transcribe.
php?uid='.$user['ID'].'&From=' . $from,
            'transcribe' => 'true'
        ));
        print $response;
        exit;
    }

});


$app->route('/transcribe', function() use ($app){
    header("Content-type: text/xml");
    $uid = $_GET['uid'];
    if( $user = get_user( $uid ) ){
        $filter     = "!@#$^&%*()+=-[]\/{}|:<>?,.";
        $recording = preg_replace("/[$filter]/", "", $_
POST['RecordingUrl']);
        $transcript = preg_replace("/[$filter]/", "", $_
POST['TranscriptionText']);
        $from    = preg_replace("/[^0-9]/", "", $_GET['From']);
        $subject = "You have a new voicemail transcription from " . $from;
        $body = "You received voicemail." .
```

```
                     "\n\nHere is the recording: $recording" .
                     "\n\nAnd here is the transcription:\n $transcript";
    mail($user['email'], $subject, $body);
    exit;
  }
});

$app->route('/call', function() use ($app){
  $app->condition('signed_in');
  $uid = $app->store('user');
  $user = get_user( $uid );
  $client = new Services_Twilio($user['sid'], $user['token']);
  $pdo = Db::singleton();
  $sql = "SELECT * FROM numbers WHERE user_id='{$user['ID']}' LIMIT
1;";
  $res = $pdo->query( $sql );
  $number = $res->fetch();
  $fromNumber = $number['number'];
  $toNumber = $user['phone_number'];
  $call = $client->account->calls->create($fromNumber, $toNumber, '/
callback?number=' . $_REQUEST['number']);

});
$app->route('/callback', function() use ($app){
    header("content-type: text/xml");
    echo "<?xml version=\"1.0\" encoding=\"UTF-8\"?>\n";
?>
<Response>
    <Say>A person at the number <?php echo $_REQUEST['number']?> is
calling</Say>
    <Dial><?php echo $_REQUEST['number']?></Dial>
</Response>
<?php
});
$app->get('/logout', function() use ($app){
        $app->store('user',0);
        $app->redirect( $app->getBaseUri().'/login');
});
$app->get('/home', function() use ($app){
  $app->condition('signed_in');
  $uid = $app->store('user');
  $user = get_user( $uid );
  $client = new Services_Twilio($user['sid'], $user['token']);
  $app->render('dashboard',array(
```

```php
      'user'=>$user,
      'client'=>$client
  ));
});
$app->get('/delete', function() use ($app){
  $app->condition('signed_in');
});
$app->get('/', function() use ($app){
  $app->render( 'home' );
});
$app->listen();
```

How it works...

In step 1, we updated `index.php` to include the `/call` and `/callback` requests.

The `/call` request handles all outgoing calls; it works by acting as a "Click-to-Call" feature, like the one we built in *Chapter 1*, *Into the Frying Pan*, where the user clicks a phone number and the system then dials the user's phone followed by the caller's phone.

Deleting a subaccount

Ok, your user has chosen to delete his account. That's fine; let's handle how to make that work.

Getting ready

The complete source code for this recipe can be found in the `Chapter9/Recipe7` folder in the source code for this book.

How to do it...

Our final recipe will walk you through how to delete a user's account. This will be done by updating the `index.php` file—for the last time—to the following content:

```php
<?php
session_start();
include 'Services/Twilio.php';
require("system/jolt.php");
require("system/pdo.class.php");
require("system/functions.php");

$_GET['route'] = isset($_GET['route']) ? '/'.$_GET['route'] : '/';
```

```
$app = new Jolt('site',false);
$app->option('source', 'config.ini');
#$pdo = Db::singleton();
$mysiteURL = $app->option('site.url');

$app->condition('signed_in', function () use ($app) {
        $app->redirect( $app->getBaseUri().'/login',!$app-
>store('user'));
});

$app->get('/login', function() use ($app){
        $app->render( 'login', array(),'layout' );
});
$app->post('/login', function() use ($app){
  $sql = "SELECT * FROM `user` WHERE `email`='{$_POST['user']}' AND
`password`='{$_POST['pass']}'";
  $pdo = Db::singleton();
  $res = $pdo->query( $sql );
  $user = $res->fetch();
  if( isset($user['ID']) ){
    $_SESSION['uid'] = $user['ID'];
    $app->store('user',$user['ID']);
        $app->redirect( $app->getBaseUri().'/home');
    }else{
        $app->redirect( $app->getBaseUri().'/login');
    }
});
$app->get('/signup', function() use ($app){
        $app->render( 'register', array(),'layout' );
});
$app->post('/signup', function() use ($app){
  $client = new Services_Twilio($app->store('twilio.accountsid'),
$app->store('twilio.authtoken') );
  extract($_POST);
  $timestamp = strtotime( $timestamp );
  $subaccount = $client->accounts->create(array(
    "FriendlyName" => $email
  ));
  $sid = $subaccount->sid;
  $token = $subaccount->auth_token;
  $sql = "INSERT INTO 'user' SET `name`='{$name}',`email`='{$email}',`
password`='{$password}',`phone_number`='{$phone_number}',`sid`='{$sid}
',`token`='{$token}',`status`=1";
  $pdo = Db::singleton();
  $pdo->exec($sql);
```

```
    $uid = $pdo->lastInsertId();
    $app->store('user',$uid );
    //  log user in
      $app->redirect( $app->getBaseUri().'/phone-number');
});
$app->get('/phone-number', function() use ($app){
  $app->condition('signed_in');
  $user = $app->store('user');
  $client = new Services_Twilio($user['sid'], $user['token']);
  $app->render('phone-number');
});

$app->post("search", function() use ($app){
  $app->condition('signed_in');
  $user = get_user( $app->store('user') );
  $client = new Services_Twilio($user['sid'], $user['token']);
  $SearchParams = array();
  $SearchParams['InPostalCode'] = !empty($_POST['postal_code']) ?
trim($_POST['postal_code']) : '';
  $SearchParams['NearNumber'] = !empty($_POST['near_number']) ?
trim($_POST['near_number']) : '';
  $SearchParams['Contains'] = !empty($_POST['contains'])? trim($_
POST['contains']) : '' ;
  try {
    $numbers = $client->account->available_phone_numbers-
>getList('US', 'Local', $SearchParams);
    if(empty($numbers)) {
      $err = urlencode("We didn't find any phone numbers by that
search");
      $app->redirect( $app->getBaseUri().'/phone-number?msg='.$err);
      exit(0);
    }
  } catch (Exception $e) {
    $err = urlencode("Error processing search: {$e->getMessage()}");
    $app->redirect( $app->getBaseUri().'/phone-number?msg='.$err);
    exit(0);
  }
  $app->render('search',array('numbers'=>$numbers));
});

$app->post("buy", function() use ($app){
  $app->condition('signed_in');
  $user = get_user( $app->store('user') );
  $client = new Services_Twilio($user['sid'], $user['token']);
  $PhoneNumber = $_POST['PhoneNumber'];
```

```php
  try {
    $number = $client->account->incoming_phone_numbers->create(array(
      'PhoneNumber' => $PhoneNumber
    ));
    $phsid = $number->sid;
    if ( !empty($phsid) ){
      $sql = "INSERT INTO numbers (user_id,number,sid) VALUES('{$user[
'ID']}','{$PhoneNumber}','{$phsid}');";
      $pdo = Db::singleton();
      $pdo->exec($sql);
      $fid = $pdo->lastInsertId();
      $ret = editNumber($phsid,array(
        "FriendlyName"=>$PhoneNumber,
        "VoiceUrl" => $mysiteURL."/voice?id=".$fid,
        "VoiceMethod" => "POST",
      ),$user['sid'], $user['token']);
    }
  } catch (Exception $e) {
    $err = urlencode("Error purchasing number: {$e->getMessage()}");
    $app->redirect( $app->getBaseUri().'/phone-number?msg='.$err);
    exit(0);
  }
  $msg = urlencode("Thank you for purchasing $PhoneNumber");
  header("Location: index.php?msg=$msg");
  $app->redirect( $app->getBaseUri().'/home?msg='.$msg);
  exit(0);
});

$app->route('/voice', function() use ($app){
  header("Content-type: text/xml");
  $fid = $_GET['id'];
  $from = preg_replace("/[^0-9]/", "", $_POST['From']);
  $pdo = Db::singleton();
  $sql = "SELECT * FROM numbers WHERE ID='{$fid}';";
  $res = $pdo->query( $sql );
  $number = $res->fetch();
  $fromNumber = $number['number'];
  if( $user = get_user($number['user_id']) ){
    $_SESSION['uid'] = $user['ID'];
    $toNumber = $user['phone_number'];
    $name = $user['name'];
    $response = new Services_Twilio_Twiml();
    $response->dial($toNumber, array('timeout' => 5));
```

```
        $response->say("I'm sorry, $name is not available at this time.
Please leave a message after the tone.");
        $response->record(array(
            'transcribeCallback' => 'transcribe.
php?uid='.$user['ID'].'&From=' . $from,
            'transcribe' => 'true'
        ));
        print $response;
        exit;
    }

});


$app->route('/transcribe', function() use ($app){
    header("Content-type: text/xml");
    $uid = $_GET['uid'];
    if( $user = get_user( $uid ) ){
        $filter     = "!@#$^&%*()+=-[]\/{}|:<>?,.";
        $recording  = preg_replace("/[$filter]/", "", $_
POST['RecordingUrl']);
        $transcript = preg_replace("/[$filter]/", "", $_
POST['TranscriptionText']);
        $from    = preg_replace("/[^0-9]/", "", $_GET['From']);
        $subject = "You have a new voicemail transcription from " . $from;
        $body = "You received voicemail." .
                "\n\nHere is the recording: $recording" .
                "\n\nAnd here is the transcription:\n $transcript";
        mail($user['email'], $subject, $body);
        exit;
    }
});

$app->route('/call', function() use ($app){
    $app->condition('signed_in');
    $uid = $app->store('user');
    $user = get_user( $uid );
    $client = new Services_Twilio($user['sid'], $user['token']);
    $pdo = Db::singleton();
    $sql = "SELECT * FROM numbers WHERE user_id='{$user['ID']}' LIMIT
1;";
    $res = $pdo->query( $sql );
    $number = $res->fetch();
    $fromNumber = $number['number'];
    $toNumber = $user['phone_number'];
```

```
    $call = $client->account->calls->create($fromNumber, $toNumber, '/
callback?number=' . $_REQUEST['number']);

});
$app->route('/callback', function() use ($app){
    header("content-type: text/xml");
    echo "<?xml version=\"1.0\" encoding=\"UTF-8\"?>\n";
?>
<Response>
    <Say>A person at the number <?php echo $_REQUEST['number']?> is
calling</Say>
    <Dial><?php echo $_REQUEST['number']?></Dial>
</Response>
<?php
});
$app->get('/logout', function() use ($app){
        $app->store('user',0);
        $app->redirect( $app->getBaseUri().'/login');
});
$app->get('/home', function() use ($app){
  $app->condition('signed_in');
  $uid = $app->store('user');
  $user = get_user( $uid );
  $client = new Services_Twilio($user['sid'], $user['token']);
  $app->render('dashboard',array(
    'user'=>$user,
    'client'=>$client
  ));
});
$app->get('/delete', function() use ($app){
  $app->condition('signed_in');
  $uid = $app->store('user');
  $user = get_user( $uid );
  $client = new Services_Twilio($user['sid'], $user['token']);
  $pdo = Db::singleton();
  $sql = "SELECT * FROM numbers WHERE user_id='{$user['ID']}';";
  $res = $pdo->query( $sql );
  while( $number = $res->fetch() ){
    releaseNumber($user['sid'],$user['token'],$number['sid'])
  }
  $account = $client->accounts->get($user['sid']);
  $account->update(array(
    "Status" => "closed"
  ));
```

```
$sql = "DELETE FROM numbers WHERE user_id='{$user['ID']}';";
$pdo->exec($sql);
$sql = "DELETE FROM user WHERE ID='{$user['ID']}';";
$pdo->exec($sql);
    $app->store('user',0);
    $app->redirect( $app->getBaseUri().'/login');
});
$app->get('/', function() use ($app){
  $app->render( 'home' );
});
$app->listen();
```

How it works...

In this recipe, we updated `index.php` to add a new route called `/delete`.

This new route performs the following operations:

- First, it releases the phone numbers the user may have registered
- Second, it closes the user's subaccount
- Third, it deletes his/her numbers from our database
- Finally, it deletes the user's record from our database

This function is pretty powerful, so it only works for the user currently logged in.

10
Digging into OpenVBX

In this chapter, you will learn the following operations:

- ► Building a call log plugin
- ► Building a searchable company directory
- ► Collecting Stripe payments
- ► Tracking orders
- ► Building a caller ID routing plugin
- ► Testing call flows

Introduction

In this last chapter will be digging into OpenVBX.

OpenVBX is an open source VBX system built by Twilio that you can use to quickly set up your calls.

I like to use OpenVBX for various projects because it allows for a rapid setup and your users can use it to handle incoming calls, outgoing calls, and messages. This has an easy-to-learn drag-and-drop call flow system.

We'll be building plugins to extend our OpenVBX installation so that you can make it more useful to your users.

By the end of the chapter, you'll have a nice call log and a searchable company directory. You will be able to collect Stripe payments over the phone, have a handy order status tracking system integrated into your site, have a caller ID, and finally, be able to test your call flows.

Flows are what the call workflows are known as; they can be set up as easily as dragging a box onto action.

As part of building our plugins, we'll also be building what OpenVBX refers to as **applets**, which are the actionable items we can drop into a call flow.

The file structures of plugins are such that, inside the `plugins` folder, you'll create a folder for your new plugin. Inside that folder you will create a `plugin.json` file that contains metadata about your plugin.

If your plugin uses applets, which are the boxes you can use for adding a plugin into a call flow, you will also create an `applets` folder inside your `plugin` folder; then inside that folder you will create a folder with the name of the applet.

Inside each `applet` folder, you will have a file called `applet.json`, a file called `ui.php` that handles the actual UI of the applet, and finally a file called `twiml.php` that handles the actual call instructions and tells the applet what it needs to do when activated.

This way, you could have multiple applets for one plugin, if you want to.

Go ahead and install OpenVBX so you can play with this cool system.

Building a call log plugin

This is a basic plugin that is a good starting point for you.

We're going to build a call log that will add a menu option to the side menu and, when clicked, will show us recent calls.

Getting ready

The complete source code for this recipe can be found in `Chapter10/Recipe1` in the source code for this book.

How to do it...

We're going to build a basic call logging system. This will give us a call log on the menu of our OpenVBX install, which we can then use to view account usage. The following are the steps you will need to perform:

1. Create a folder in your `plugins` folder, and name it `calllog`.

2. Create a file named `plugin.json` and write in the following code:

   ```
   {
      "name" : "Call Log",
      "description" : "This displays a list of all the calls and sms
   that have been made or received.",
      "links" : [{
         "menu" : "Call Log",
   ```

```
    "url" : "call_log",
    "script" : "call_log.php",
    "label" : "Call Log"
  }]
}
```

3. Create a file named `call_log.php` and write in the following code:

```php
<?php

classcall_log{
  private $limit;
  private $account;
  public function __construct($limit = 20){
    $this->limit = $limit;
    $this->account = OpenVBX::getAccount();
  }
  public function list_calls(){
    $calls = $this->account->calls->getPage(0, $this->limit,
array())->getItems();
?>
    <div class="vbx-plugin">
    <h3>Call Log</h3>
    <p>Showing the last <?= $this->limit; ?> calls.</p>
    <table>
    <thead>
    <tr>
      <th>Number</th>
      <th>Start Time</th>
      <th>End Time</th>
      <th>Duration</th>
      <th>Called</th>
      <th>Status</th>
    </tr>
    </thead>
    <tbody>
    <?php  foreach($calls as $call){ ?>
    <tr>
      <td><?= $this->who_called($call->from); ?></td>
      <td><?= $this->nice_date($call->start_time); ?></td>
      <td><?= $this->nice_date($call->end_time); ?></td>
      <td><?=gmdate("H:i:s",$call->duration); ?></td>
      <td><?= $this->who_called($call->to); ?></td>
      <td><?= $this->be_nice($call->status); ?></td>
    </tr>
```

```php
        <?php  } ?>
        </tbody>
        </table>
        </div>
    <?php
      }
    public function be_nice($status, $sep = '-') {
      returnucwords(str_replace($sep, ' ', $status));
    }
    public function who_called($number) {
      if (preg_match('|^client:|', $number)){
      $user_id = str_replace('client:', '', $number);
        $user = VBX_User::get(array('id' => $user_id));
        $ret = $user->first_name.' '.$user->last_name.' (client)';
      }else{
        $ret = format_phone($number);
      }
      return $ret;
    }
    public function nice_date($date){
      $timestamp = strtotime($date);
      return date('M j, Y', $timestamp).'<br />'.date('H:i:s T',
$timestamp );
    }
}

$log = new call_log(50);
$log->list_calls();
```

How it works...

The call log is pretty simple but it works nicely.

The plugin used adds a menu item called **Call Log**; when the user clicks on that menu item, it will display a table containing the last fifty calls that their Twilio account has made.

Building a searchable company directory

I have received requests from people wanting to add a searchable company directory to their systems. For this, let's create a plugin that will come in handy. This plugin will also introduce you to setting up applets.

Getting ready

The complete source code for this recipe can be found at `Chapter10/Recipe2` in the source code for this book.

How to do it...

The following plugin is going to give us a searchable user directory. Perform the following steps to build the plugin:

1. Create a folder in your `plugins` folder, and name it `directory`.

2. Create a file named `plugin.json` and write in the following code:

```json
{
  "name" : "Directory",
  "description" : "Searchable directory of Users.",
}
```

3. Inside the `directory` folder, create a folder named `applets`.

4. Upload a new file called `directory.class.php` and write in the following code:

```php
<?php

class DirectorySearch{
  public function __construct(){
  }

  public function connect($response, $user){
    $name = $user->first_name . " " . $user->last_name;
    $device = $_SESSION[SESSION_KEY]['number']++;
    if(isset($user->devices[$device])){
      if(!$user->devices[$device]->is_active){
        return connect($response, $user);
      }
      $dial = $response->addDial(array('action' =>current_url()));
      $dial->addNumber($user->devices[$device]->value, array('url'
=>site_url('twiml/whisper?name='.urlencode($name))));
    } else {
    $response->append(AudioSpeechPickerWidget::getVerbForValue($us
er->voicemail, new Say("Please leave a message.")));
    $response->addRecord(array(
        'transcribe' => 'true',
        'transcribeCallback' =>site_url('twiml/transcribe') ));
    }
    return $response;
```

```
    }
    public function promptMenu($response, $users){
      $gather = $response->addGather();
      foreach($users as $index => $user){
        $pos = $index + 1;
        $gather->addSay("Dial $pos for {$user->first_name} {$user-
>last_name}");
      }
      return $response;
    }
    public function searchPrompt($response){
      unset($_SESSION[SESSION_KEY]);
      $this->addMessage($response->addGather(), 'searchPrompt',
'Please enter the first few letters of the name, followed by the
pound sign.');
      return $response;
    }
    function errorResponse($response){
      return $this->addMessage($response, 'errorMessage', 'Sorry, an
error occurred.');
    }
    public function addMessage($response, $name, $fallback){
      $message = AppletInstance::getAudioSpeechPickerValue($name);
      $response->append(AudioSpeechPickerWidget::getVerbForValue($me
ssage, new Say($fallback)));
      return $response;
    }
    public function getMatches($digits){
      $indexes = array();
      $matches = array();
      $users = OpenVBX::getUsers(array('is_active' => 1));
      foreach($users as $user) {
        $fname = $user->values['first_name'];
        $lname = $user->values['last_name'];
        $fdigits = $this->stringToDigits( $fname );
        $ldigits = $this->stringToDigits( $lname );
        if( stristr($fdigits,$digits) || stristr($ldigits,$digits) )
{
          $matches[] = $user;
        }
      }
      return $matches;
    }
    private function stringToDigits($str) {
      $str = strtolower($str);
```

```
    $from = 'abcdefghijklmnopqrstuvwxyz';
    $to = '22233344455566677778889999';
    return preg_replace('/[^0-9]/', '', strtr($str, $from, $to));
  }
}
```

5. Inside the `applets` folder, create a folder and name it `directory`.

6. Create a file named `applet.json` and write in the following code:

```json
{
    "name" : "Directory Search",
    "description" : "Search Directory of users",
    "type" : "voice"
}
```

7. Create a file named `ui.php` and write in the following code:

```php
<div class="vbx-applet">
<h2>Directory Search</h2>
<p>Callers can search for users by dialing a few letters of the
user's first or last name. They can press pound when done, or
simply wait for 5 seconds. </p>
<h3>Search Prompt</h3>
<p>When the caller reaches this menu they will hear this prompt:</
p>
<?=AppletUI::audioSpeechPicker('searchMenu'); ?>
<h3>Menu Prompt</h3>
<p>The caller can select a user from the menu, or dial 0 to try
again. Before the user menu is played, play this prompt:</p>
<?=AppletUI::audioSpeechPicker('dirMenu'); ?>
<h3>No Matches</h3>
<p>Select a message to play when no users are found, before the
process is restarted.</p>
<?=AppletUI::audioSpeechPicker('nomatchMessage'); ?>
<h3>Restart Search</h3>
<p>The caller dialed 0 to restart the search, customize this
message.</p>
<?=AppletUI::audioSpeechPicker('restartMessage'); ?>
<h3>Invalid Selection</h3>
<p>Customize a specific message about the invalid selection.</p>
<?=AppletUI::audioSpeechPicker('invalidMessage'); ?>
<h3>Error Message</h3>
<p>Pick a message to notify the caller an error occurred before
the process is restarted.</p>
<?=AppletUI::audioSpeechPicker('errorMessage'); ?>
</div>
```

8. Upload a file called `twiml.php`, bearing the following code:

```php
<?php
require_once(dirname(dirname(dirname(__FILE__))) . '/directory.
class.php');
include_once(APPPATH.'models/vbx_device.php');
define('SESSION_KEY', AppletInstance::getInstanceId());
session_start();

$directory = new DirectorySearch();

if(isset($_SESSION[SESSION_KEY]['user'])){
  $user = unserialize($_SESSION[SESSION_KEY]['user']);
  if(isset($_REQUEST['RecordingUrl'])){
    OpenVBX::addVoiceMessage(
      $user,
      $_REQUEST['CallGuid'],
      $_REQUEST['Caller'],
      $_REQUEST['Called'],
      $_REQUEST['RecordingUrl'],
      $_REQUEST['Duration']);

    $response = new Response();
    $response->addHangup();
    $response->Respond();
    return;
  } elseif(isset($_REQUEST['DialStatus']) OR isset($_
REQUEST['DialCallStatus'])) {
    if(!isset($_REQUEST['DialStatus'])){
     $_REQUEST['DialStatus'] = $_REQUEST['DialCallStatus'];
    }
    if('answered' == $_REQUEST['DialStatus']){
      $response = new Response();
      $response->addHangup();
      $response->Respond();
      return;
    }
    return $directory->connect(new Response(), $user)->Respond();
  }
  return $directory->searchPrompt($directory->errorResponse(new
Response()))->Respond();
}
if(isset($_SESSION[SESSION_KEY]['users'])) {
  $users = unserialize($_SESSION[SESSION_KEY]['users']);
  $index = $_REQUEST['Digits'];
```

```
    if("0" == $index){
        return $directory->searchPrompt($directory->addMessage(new
Response(), 'restartMessage', 'Starting over.'))->Respond();
    } elseif(!isset($users[$index - 1])){
        return $directory->promptMenu($directory->addMessage(new
Response(), 'invalidMessage', 'Not a valid selection.'), $users)-
>Respond();
    }
    unset($_SESSION[SESSION_KEY]['users']);
    $user = $users[$index - 1];
    $_SESSION[SESSION_KEY]['user'] = serialize($user);
    $_SESSION[SESSION_KEY]['number'] = 0;
    $response = new Response();
    $response->addSay("Connecting you to {$user->first_name} {$user-
>last_name}");
    return $directory->connect($response, $user)->Respond();
}
if(isset($_REQUEST['Digits'])){
    $users = $directory->getMatches($_REQUEST['Digits']);
    if(0 == count($users)){
        return $directory->searchPrompt($directory->addMessage(new
Response(), 'nomatchMessage', 'Sorry, no matches found.'))-
>Respond();
    }
    $_SESSION[SESSION_KEY]['users'] = serialize($users);
    return $directory->promptMenu($directory->addMessage(new
Response(), 'menuPrompt', 'Please select a user, or press 0 to
search again.'), $users)->Respond();
}
return $directory->searchPrompt(new Response())->Respond();
```

How it works...

In step 1, we created a folder called `directory`. In step 2, we created our `plugin.json` file.

Step 3 saw us upload `directory.class.php`, the actual brain of our plugin.

In steps 4 and 5, we created an `applets` folder and then a folder called `directory` inside it. In step 6, we created `applet.json`.

Finally in steps 7 and 8, we created our `ui.php` and `twiml.php` files that tell the plugin's applet how to look and act when used in a call flow.

When the user opens up OpenVBX, they can choose an applet that can be used in a call flow. Choosing **Directory Search** will present them with a box to add actions; this is defined in `ui.php`.

When a call is made and the directory is triggered, then we use `twiml.php` to tell the system what to do. In this case, we prompt the system to search for any user who matches the digits we enter. So, typing `787` will find a match for **Stringer** and will attempt to call me.

You may notice that the `stringToDigits` function we originally used in our company directory has returned. That's because this is a perfect example of matching a name based on phone digits.

Collecting Stripe payments

At some point in most projects, you will want a way to collect payments. This recipe will show you how to set up payments via Stripe and give your users a set of prompts where they can enter their credit card information in order to conduct the payment.

Getting ready

The complete source code for this recipe can be found at `Chapter10/Recipe3` in the source code for this book.

How to do it...

We're going to build a plugin that will let users make stripe payments over the phone. Perform the following steps to do so:

1. Download the latest version of the Stripe API for PHP from `https://code.stripe.com/stripe-php-latest.zip`.

2. Create a folder in your `plugins/` folder of your OpenVBX installation, name it `stripe`, and upload the `stripe-php` folder.

3. Upload a file on your server called `plugin.json` with the following content:

```json
{
  "name" : "Stripe",
  "description" : "Take payments over the phone using stripe.com",
  "links" : [{
    "menu" : "Stripe",
    "url" : "stripe",
    "script" : "stripe.php",
    "label" : "Settings"
  }]
}
```

4. Upload a file on your server called `script.js` with the following content:

```
$(function() {
  $('.vbx-stripe :checkbox').click(function() {
    $('.vbx-stripe form p').eq(5).slideToggle();
  });
  if(!$('.vbx-stripe :checked').length)
    $('.vbx-stripe form p').eq(5).hide();
});
```

5. Upload a file on your server called `stripe.php` with the following content:

```php
<?php
if(count($_POST)){
PluginData::set('settings', array(
    'api_key' => $_POST['api_key'],
    'card_prompt' => $_POST['card_prompt'],
    'month_prompt' => $_POST['month_prompt'],
    'year_prompt' => $_POST['year_prompt'],
    'require_cvc' =>isset($_POST['require_cvc']),
    'cvc_prompt' => $_POST['cvc_prompt']
  ));
}
$settings = PluginData::get('settings', array(
  'api_key' => null,
  'card_prompt' => "Please enter your credit card number followed
by the pound sign.",
  'month_prompt' => "Please enter the month of the card's
expiration date followed by the pound sign.",
  'year_prompt' => "Please enter the year of the expiration date
followed by the pound sign.",
  'require_cvc' => true,
  'cvc_prompt' => "Please enter the card's security code followed
by the pound sign."
));
OpenVBX::addJS('script.js');
?>
<div class="vbx-content-main">
<div class="vbx-content-menu vbx-content-menu-top">
<h2 class="vbx-content-heading">Stripe Settings</h2>
</div>
<div class="vbx-table-section vbx-stripe">
<form method="post" action="">
<fieldset class="vbx-input-container">
<p>
<label class="field-label">API Key<br/>
```

```
<input type="password" name="api_key" class="medium" value="<?=
htmlentities($settings->api_key); ?>" />
</label>
</p>
<p>Please enter what you want to say to your customer as they fill
out your order form over the phone.</p>
<p>
<label class="field-label">Credit card prompt<br/>
<textarea rows="10" cols="100" name="card_prompt"
class="medium"><?= htmlentities($settings->card_prompt); ?></
textarea>
</label>
</p>
<p>
<label class="field-label">Expiration month prompt<br/>
<textarea rows="10" cols="100" name="month_prompt"
class="medium"><?= htmlentities($settings->month_prompt); ?></
textarea>
</label>
</p>
<p>
<label class="field-label">Expiration year prompt<br/>
<textarea rows="10" cols="100" name="year_prompt"
class="medium"><?= htmlentities($settings->year_prompt); ?></
textarea>
</label>
</p>
<p>
<label class="field-label">
<input type="checkbox" name="require_cvc" <?= $settings->require_
cvc ? ' checked="checked"' : ''; ?> /> Require CVC
</label>
</p>
<p>
<label class="field-label">Card CVC prompt<br/>
<textarea rows="10" cols="100" name="cvc_prompt"
class="medium"><?= htmlentities($settings->cvc_prompt); ?></
textarea>
</label>
</p>
<p><button type="submit" class="submit-button"><span>Save</span></
button></p>
</fieldset>
</form>
</div>
</div>
```

6. In your `stripe` folder, create a folder and name it `applets`.

7. In the `applets` folder, create another folder and name it `stripe`.

8. In the `stripe` folder, create an `applet.json` file with the following content:

```
{
   "name" : "Payment",
   "sms_name" : "Payment",
   "voice_title" : "Payment",
   "sms_title" : "Payment",
   "description" : "Take a credit card payment.",
   "type" : "voice"
}
```

9. Create a file named `ui.php` and write in the following code:

```php
<?php
  $settings = PluginData::get('settings');
  if(is_object($settings)){
    $settings = get_object_vars($settings);
  }
?>
<div class="vbx-applet">
<?php if( empty($settings) || empty($settings['api_key'])){ ?>
  <div class="vbx-full-pane">
    <h3><em>Please set your Stripe.com settings first.</em></h3>
  </div>
<?php }else{ ?>
  <div class="vbx-full-pane">
    <h3>Amount to charge in cents?</h3>
    <p>How much money in cents to charge the card <small>($5.00
would be 500 cents)</small>.</p>
    <fieldset class="vbx-input-container">
      <input type="text" name="amount" class="medium" value="<?php
echo AppletInstance::getValue('amount', 50); ?>" />
    </fieldset>
    <h3>What they are paying for?</h3>
    <fieldset class="vbx-input-container">
      <input type="text" name="description" class="medium"
value="<?php echo AppletInstance::getValue('description'); ?>" />
    </fieldset>
  </div>
  <h2>What to do after the payment</h2>
  <div class="vbx-full-pane">
    <?php echo AppletUI::DropZone('success'); ?>
  </div>
  <h2>If the payment fails</h2>
```

```
    <div class="vbx-full-pane">
      <?php echo AppletUI::DropZone('fail'); ?>
    </div>
  <?php } ?>
</div>
```

10. Lastly, create a file and name it `twiml.php`, containing the following code:

```php
<?php
$const = array();
$const['STRIPE_ACTION'] = 'stripeAction';
$const['STRIPE_COOKIE'] =  'payment-' . AppletInstance::getInstanc
eId();
$const['GATHER_CARD'] =  'GatherCard';
$const['GATHER_MONTH'] =  'GatherMonth';
$const['GATHER_YEAR'] =  'GatherYear';
$const['GATHER_CVC'] =  'GatherCvc';
$const['SEND_PAYMENT'] =  'SendPayment';
foreach($const as $k=>$v){
  define($k,$v);
}

$response = new TwimlResponse;

$state = array(
  STRIPE_ACTION => GATHER_CARD,
  'card' => array()
);

$ci =&get_instance();
$settings = PluginData::get('settings');
$amount = AppletInstance::getValue('amount');
$description = AppletInstance::getValue('description');
$digits = clean_digits($ci->input->get_post('Digits'));
$finishOnKey = '#';
$timeout = 15;

$card_errors = array(
  'invalid_number' => GATHER_CARD,
  'incorrect_number' => GATHER_CARD,
  'invalid_expiry_month' => GATHER_MONTH,
  'invalid_expiry_year' => GATHER_YEAR,
  'expired_card' => GATHER_CARD,
  'invalid_cvc' => GATHER_CVC,
  'incorrect_cvc' => GATHER_CVC
```

```
);

if(is_object($settings))   $settings = get_object_vars($settings);

if(isset($_COOKIE[STRIPE_COOKIE])) {
  $state = json_decode(str_replace(', $Version=0', '', $_
COOKIE[STRIPE_COOKIE]), true);
  if(is_object($state))    $state = get_object_vars($state);
}

if($digits !== false) {
  switch($state[STRIPE_ACTION]) {
    case GATHER_CARD:
      $state['card']['number'] = $digits;
      $state[STRIPE_ACTION] = GATHER_MONTH;
      break;
    case GATHER_MONTH:
      $state['card']['exp_month'] = $digits;
      $state[STRIPE_ACTION] = GATHER_YEAR;
      break;
    case GATHER_YEAR:
      $state['card']['exp_year'] = $digits;
      $state[STRIPE_ACTION] = $settings['require_cvc'] ? GATHER_
CVC : SEND_PAYMENT;
      break;
    case GATHER_CVC:
      $state['card']['cvc'] = $digits;
      $state[STRIPE_ACTION] = SEND_PAYMENT;
      break;
  }
}
switch($state[STRIPE_ACTION]) {
  case GATHER_CARD:
  default:
    $gather = $response->gather(compact('finishOnKey',
'timeout'));
    $gather->addSay($settings['card_prompt']);
    break;
  case GATHER_MONTH:
    $gather = $response->gather(compact('finishOnKey',
'timeout'));
    $gather->addSay($settings['month_prompt']);
    break;
  case GATHER_YEAR:
```

```
    $gather = $response->gather(compact('finishOnKey',
'timeout'));
    $gather->addSay($settings['year_prompt']);
    break;
  case GATHER_CVC:
    $gather = $response->gather(compact('finishOnKey',
'timeout'));
    $gather->addSay($settings['cvc_prompt']);
    break;
  case SEND_PAYMENT:
    require_once(dirname(dirname(dirname(__FILE__))) . '/stripe-
php/lib/Stripe.php');
    Stripe::setApiKey($settings['api_key']);
    try {
      $charge = Stripe_Charge::create(array(
        'card' => $state['card'],
        'amount' => $amount,
        'currency' => 'usd',
        'description' => $description
      ));
      if($charge->paid && true === $charge->paid) {
        setcookie(STRIPE_COOKIE);
        $next = AppletInstance::getDropZoneUrl('success');
        if(!empty($next))  $response->redirect($next);
        $response->respond();
        die;
      }
    }catch(Exception $e) {
      $error = $e->getCode();
      $response->addSay($e->getMessage());
      if(array_key_exists($error, $card_errors)) {
        $state[STRIPE_ACTION] = $card_errors[$error];
        $response->redirect();
      }else {
        setcookie(STRIPE_COOKIE);
        $next = AppletInstance::getDropZoneUrl('fail');
        if(!empty($next))  $response->redirect($next);
        $response->respond();
        die;
      }
    }
}
setcookie(STRIPE_COOKIE, json_encode($state), time() + (5 * 60));
$response->respond();
```

How it works...

In step 1, we downloaded the Stripe API library for PHP.

In step 2, we created a folder called `stripe`; then, in step 3, we created our `plugin.json` file.

In steps 4 and 5, we created `script.js` and `stripe.php`. This lets us set up our initial Stripe account information.

In steps 6 and 7, we created an `applets` folder and then a folder called `stripe` inside the `applets` folder. Then, in step 8, we created `applet.json`.

Finally, in steps 9 and 10, we created our `ui.php` and `twiml.php` files. These files tell the plugin's applet how to look and act when used in a call flow.

In our **Settings** menu, we have the ability to enter in our Stripe data.

When we add Stripe to our call flows, we have the ability to enter in a product or service name and how much to charge for it.

Now, when someone calls into a call flow that has Stripe added to it, they will get a set of prompts to purchase an item.

First, they will enter their credit card number, their cards' expiry month, and the expiry year; then it will prompt for the caller to enter his/her CVC number.

Finally, the plugin will send the information to Stripe and process the payment. If it succeeds, they will get a success message.

A good example of this would be to configure the work flow so that each menu option or extension triggers the purchase of a different product or service.

Tracking orders

Yes, this is another order status tracking recipe. But this one will demonstrate how to use it inside OpenVBX.

This order tracker will let us create a page where you can enter in orders and their statuses and also incorporate the tracking into call flows.

For example, if we were setting up an IVR-type system, pressing 2 might load the order tracking code and prompt the user to enter in their order ID.

The complete source code for this recipe can be found at `Chapter10/Recipe4` in the source code for this book.

Let's build an order tracking system into our OpenVBX plugin now. We're going to set up an interface to store order IDs and statuses; then we'll perform a look-up of those orders when people call in. Perform the following steps to do so:

1. Create a folder in your `plugins` folder and name it `orders`.

2. Create a file and name it `plugin.json`, containing the following code:

```json
{
  "name" : "Orders",
  "description" : "Allows order tracking over the phone",
  "links" : [{
    "menu" : "Order Tracker",
    "url" : "orders",
    "script" : "orders.php",
    "label" : "Orders"
  }]
}
```

3. Upload a file called `orders.php`, bearing the following code:

```php
<?php
if(count($_POST)){
  foreach($_POST['keys'] as $k=>$v){
    if( empty($v) ){
      unset( $_POST['keys'][$k] );
      unset( $_POST['status'][$k] );
    }
  }
  PluginData::set('orders', array(
    'keys' => $_POST['keys'],
    'status' => $_POST['status'],
  ));
}
$settings = PluginData::get('orders', array(
  'keys' => array(),
  'status' => array(),
));
$statusArray = array(
```

```
    'shipped'=>'Shipped',
    'fullfillment'=>'Sent to Fullfillment',
    'processing'=>'Processing'
);
OpenVBX::addJS('script.js');
?>
<div class="vbx-plugin orders-applet">
<form method="post">
  <h2>Order Tracker</h2>
  <p>Enter an order ID, without spaces.  For example, <code>1234</
code> instead of <code>123 4</code>.</p>
  <table class="vbx-orders-grid options-table">
  <thead>
    <tr>
      <td>Order ID</td>
      <td>Status</td>
      <td>Actions</td>
    </tr>
  </thead>
  <tbody>
    <?php foreach($settings->keys as $i=>$key){ ?>
    <tr>
      <td>
        <fieldset class="vbx-input-container">
          <input class="keypress" type="text" name="keys[]"
value="<?php echo $key ?>" autocomplete="off" />
        </fieldset>
      </td>
<td>
        <select name="status[]">
<?php
        foreach($statusArray as $k=>$v){
          $sel = '';
          if( $settings->status[ $i ] == $k )  $sel = 'SELECTED';
?>
          <option value="<?=$k?>" <?=$sel?>><?=$v?></option>
<?php
        }
?>
        </select>
      </td>
      <td>
        <a href="" class="add action"><span
class="replace">Update</span></a><a href="" class="remove
action"><span class="replace">Remove</span></a>
```

```
                </td>
            </tr>
            <?php } ?>
        </tbody>
        <tfoot>
            <tr>
                <td>
                    <fieldset class="vbx-input-container">
                        <input class="keypress" type="text" name="keys[]"
value="" autocomplete="off" />
                    </fieldset>
                </td>
                <td>
                    <select name="status[]">
<?php
                    foreach($statusArray as $k=>$v){
                    $sel = '';

?>
                    <option value="<?=$k?>" <?=$sel?>><?=$v?></option>
<?php
                    }
?>
                    </select>
                </td>
                <td>
                    <a href="" class="add action"><span
class="replace">Update</span></a><a href="" class="remove
action"><span class="replace">Remove</span></a>
                </td>
            </tr>
        </tfoot>
    </table><!-- .vbx-orders-grid -->
<button type="submit">Save Orders</button>
</form>
</div><!-- .vbx-applet -->
```

4. Upload a file called `script.js`, bearing the following code:

```
$(document).ready(function() {
    $('.orders-applet tr.hide input').attr('disabled', 'disabled');
    var app = $('.flow-instance.standard---orders');
    $('.orders-applet .orders-prompt .audio-choice', app).
live('save', function(event, mode, value) {
```

```
      var text = '';
      if(mode == 'say') {
        text = value;
      } else {
        text = 'Play';
      }
      var instance = $(event.target).parents('.flow-instance.
standard---orders');
      if(text.length> 0) {
        $(instance).trigger('set-name', Order ID: ' + text.substr(0,
6) + '...');
      }
    });
  $('.orders-applet .action.add').live('click', function(event) {
      event.preventDefault();
      var row = $(this).closest('tr');
      varnewRow = $('tfoottr', $(this).parents('.orders-applet')).
html();
      newRow = $('<tr>' + newRow + '</tr>').show().insertAfter(row);
      $('td', newRow).flicker();
      $('input.keypress', newRow).attr('name', 'keys[]');
      $('input', newRow).removeAttr('disabled').focus();
      $(event.target).parents('.options-table').trigger('change');
      return false;
    });
  $('.orders-applet .action.remove').live('click', function() {
      var row = $(this).closest('tr');
      var bgColor = row.css('background-color');
      row.animate({backgroundColor : '#FEEEBD'},'fast').
fadeOut('fast', function() {
        row.remove();
      });
      return false;
    });
  $('.orders-applet .options-table').live('change', function() {
      var first = $('tbodytr', this).first();
      $('.action.remove', first).hide();
    });
  $('.orders-applet .options-table').trigger('change');
});
```

5. Create another folder called `applets`.

6. Inside the `applets` folder, create a folder and name it `orders`.

7. Inside the orders folder, create a new file, name it applet.json, and write in the following code:

```json
{
  "name" : "Orders",
  "sms_name" : "Orders",
  "voice_title" : "Orders",
  "sms_title" : "Orders",
  "description" : "Take a credit card payment.",
  "type" : ["voice","sms"]
}
```

8. Upload a file called ui.php, bearing the following code:

```php
<?php
  $flow_type = AppletInstance::getFlowType();
  $vp = AppletInstance::getValue('prompt-text');
?>
<div class="vbx-applet monkey-applet">
<h2>Order Tracking</h2>
<p>Enter  a custom message that your callers will be greeted by.</
p>
<textarea class="medium" name="prompt-text"><?php
echo ( !empty($vp) ? AppletInstance::getValue('prompt-text') :
'Please enter your order id' )
?></textarea>
<?php if($flow_type == 'voice'): ?>
  <br/>
  <h2>Next</h2>
  <p>After retrieving the order id, continue to the next applet</
p>
  <div class="vbx-full-pane">
    <?php echo AppletUI::DropZone('next'); ?>
  </div>
<?phpendif; ?>
</div>
```

9. Upload a file called twiml.php, bearing the following code:

```php
<?php
$ci =&get_instance();
$flow_type = AppletInstance::getFlowType();

if($flow_type != 'voice'){
  $orderid = $_REQUEST['Body'];
}else{
  $digits = clean_digits($ci->input->get_post('Digits'));
```

```
    if(!empty($digits))  $orderid = $digits;
}
$prefs = array(
  'voice' => $ci->vbx_settings->get('voice', $ci->tenant->id),
  'language' => $ci->vbx_settings->get('voice_language', $ci-
>tenant->id)
);

$response = new TwimlResponse;

if(!empty($orderid)) {
  $settings = PluginData::get('orders', array(
    'keys' => array(),
    'status' => array(),
  ));
  $statusArray = array(
    'shipped'=>'Shipped',
    'fullfillment'=>'Sent to Fullfillment',
    'processing'=>'Processing'
  );
  $s = '';
  $keys = $settings->keys;
  $status = $settings->status;
  foreach($keys as $i=>$key ){
    if( $key == $orderid ){
      $s = $statusArray[ $status[$i] ];
      break;
    }
  }
  if( $s != '' ){
    $response->say("Your order is marked as {$s}.", $prefs);
    if(AppletInstance::getFlowType() == 'voice') {
      $next = AppletInstance::getDropZoneUrl('next');
      if(!empty($next))  $response->redirect($next);
    }
  }else{
    $response->say("We could not find your order.", $prefs);
  }
}elseif($flow_type == 'voice' ) {
  $gather = $response->gather(array('numDigits' => 5));
  $gather->say( AppletInstance::getValue('prompt-text'), $prefs );
  $response->redirect();
}elseif($flow_type != 'voice' ) {
  $response->say( AppletInstance::getValue('prompt-text') );
}

$response->respond();
```

How it works...

In step 1, we created the `orders` folder.

In step 2, we uploaded `plugin.json`; in steps 3 and 4, we created `orders.php` and `script.js`.

In steps 5 and 6, we created the `applets` and `orders` folders.

In step 7, we created the `applet.json` file.

In step 8, we created the `ui.php` file that tells people what options they have when they add the order tracker to their call flow. In step 9, we took care of `twiml.php` that tells OpenVBX how to handle the calls.

When we log in to OpenVBX now, there will be a menu option called **Orders**, where we can enter an order ID and a status. This can be edited at any time.

When the order tracker is added to a call flow, the only option we give users is to change the message prompting callers to enter their order ID. If the call flow is a voice flow, they can also add another option to the page.

When an order ID is received, `twiml.php` will loop through the list of orders until it finds a match; then it will return a message with the status of the order.

Building a caller ID routing plugin

This simple caller ID plugin will let your user assign caller IDs to incoming phone numbers.

We're going to limit this to call flows, so that you can have the caller ID handled differently for each option in a call flow.

For example, if you set up extensions, you could say, if the extension is 1 and the call is coming from 1234567890, forward the call to voice mail; however, if the extension is 2 and the call is coming from 1234567890, call a sales person.

Getting ready

The complete source code for this recipe can be found in the `Chapter10/Recipe5` folder in the source code for this book.

How to do it...

Now let's set up a caller ID system. This system will let us define a set of actions based on the caller's phone number. So, for example, you could set it so that when your Mom calls, the system sends her directly to voice mail. Use the following steps to do so:

1. In the `plugins` folder, create a folder and name it `callerid`.

2. Within the `callerid` folder, create another folder and name it `applets`.

3. Now, within the `applets` folder, create a folder and name it `callerid`.

4. In the `callerid` folder, upload a file called `applet.json`, bearing the following code:

```
{
    "name" : "Caller ID Router",
    "description" : "Routes the call based on caller ID",
    "type" : ["voice", "sms"]
}
```

5. Upload a file called `ui.php` with the following code:

```php
<?php
$defaultNumberOfChoices = 4;
$keys = AppletInstance::getValue('keys[]', array('1','2','3','4')
);
$choices = AppletInstance::getValue('choices[]');
?>
<div class="vbx-applet callerid-applet">
  <h2>Caller ID Router</h2>
  <p>Type phone numbers without spaces or punctuation.  For
example, <code>8005551234</code> instead of <code>(800) 555-1234</
code>.</p>
    <table class="vbx-callerid-grid options-table">
    <thead>
      <tr>
        <td>Caller ID</td>
        <td> </td>
        <td>Applet</td>
        <td>Actions</td>
      </tr>
    </thead>
    <tbody>
      <?php foreach($keys as $i=>$key){ ?>
      <tr>
        <td>
          <fieldset class="vbx-input-container">
```

```
            <input class="keypress" type="text" name="keys[]"
value="<?php echo $key ?>" autocomplete="off" />
        </fieldset>
      </td>
      <td>then</td>
      <td>
        <?php echo AppletUI::dropZone('choices['.($i).']', 'Drop
item here'); ?>
      </td>
      <td>
        <a href="" class="add action"><span class="replace">Add</
span></a><a href="" class="remove action"><span
class="replace">Remove</span></a>
      </td>
    </tr>
    <?php } ?>
  </tbody>
  <tfoot>
    <tr class="hide">
      <td>
        <fieldset class="vbx-input-container">
          <input class="keypress" type="text" name="new-keys[]"
value="" autocomplete="off" />
        </fieldset>
      </td>
      <td>then</td>
      <td>
        <?php echo AppletUI::dropZone('new-choices[]', 'Drop item
here'); ?>
      </td>
      <td>
        <a href="" class="add action"><span class="replace">Add</
span></a></a>
      </td>
    </tr>
  </tfoot>
</table><!-- .vbx-callerid-grid -->
<h3>Oops!</h3>
<p>When the caller ID is not in the above list</p>
<?php echo AppletUI::dropZone('invalid'); ?>
<br />
</div><!-- .vbx-applet -->
```

6. Upload a file called `script.js` bearing the following code:

```
$(document).ready(function() {
  $('.callerid-applet tr.hide input').attr('disabled',
'disabled');
  var app = $('.flow-instance.standard---callerid');
  $('.callerid-applet .callerid-prompt .audio-choice', app).
live('save', function(event, mode, value) {
    var text = '';
    if(mode == 'say') {
      text = value;
    } else {
      text = 'Play';
    }
    var instance = $(event.target).parents('.flow-instance.
standard---callerid');
    if(text.length> 0) {
      $(instance).trigger('set-name', 'Caller ID: ' + text.
substr(0, 6) + '...');
    }
  });
  $('.callerid-applet input.keypress').live('change',
function(event) {
    var row = $(this).parents('tr');
    $('input[name=^choices]', row).attr('name', 'keys['+$(this).
val()+']');
  });
  $('.callerid-applet .action.add').live('click', function(event)
{
    event.preventDefault();
    var row = $(this).closest('tr');
    var newRow = $('tfoottr', $(this).parents('.callerid-
applet')).html();
    newRow = $('<tr>' + newRow + '</tr>').show().insertAfter(row);
    $('.flowline-item').droppable(Flows.events.drop.options);
    $('td', newRow).flicker();
    $('.flowline-item input', newRow).attr('name', 'choices[]');
    $('input.keypress', newRow).attr('name', 'keys[]');
    $('input', newRow).removeAttr('disabled').focus();
    $(event.target).parents('.options-table').trigger('change');
    return false;
  });
  $('.callerid-applet .action.remove').live('click', function() {
    var row = $(this).closest('tr');
```

```
        var bgColor = row.css('background-color');
        row.animate({backgroundColor : '#FEEEBD'},'fast').
fadeOut('fast', function() {
            row.remove();
        });
        return false;
    });
    $('.callerid-applet .options-table').live('change', function() {
        var first = $('tbodytr', this).first();
        $('.action.remove', first).hide();
    });
    $('.callerid-applet .options-table').trigger('change');
});
```

7. Upload a file called `twiml.php`, bearing the following code:

```php
<?php
$response = new Response();
$keys = AppletInstance::getValue('keys');
$invalid = AppletInstance::getDropZoneUrl('invalid');

$selected_item = false;

$choices = AppletInstance::getDropZoneUrl('choices[]');
$keys = AppletInstance::getDropZoneValue('keys[]');
$router_items = AppletInstance::assocKeyValueCombine($keys,
$choices);

if(isset($_REQUEST['From']) && array_key_exists($_REQUEST['From'],
$router_items)){
  $routed_path = $router_items[$_REQUEST['From']];
  $response->addRedirect($routed_path);
  $response->Respond();
  exit;
}else if(isset($_REQUEST['Caller']) && array_key_exists($_
REQUEST['Caller'], $router_items)){
  $routed_path = $router_items[$_REQUEST['Caller']];
  $response->addRedirect($routed_path);
  $response->Respond();
  exit;
}else{
  if(!empty($invalid)){
      $response->addRedirect($invalid);
    $response->Respond();
    exit;
  }else{
```

```
        $response->Respond();
        exit;
    }
}
```

How it works...

In steps 1, 2, and 3, we created the folders to host the applet.

Step 4 saw the creation of the `applet.json` file.

In steps 5, 6, and 7, we created the `ui.php`, `script.js` and `twiml.php` files to tell OpenVBX how to behave.

This plugin consists entirely of an applet.

When we add the caller ID plugin to a call flow, we are presented with the ability to add a list of phone numbers. Then, choose an option for each number.

This is can be configured inside a call flow in whatever manner we want it to be. It can be at the front of a menu or behind a menu, and can help extend our OpenVBX system to an extent.

Testing call flows

We've built our various plugins and applets to create call flows. Now we want to test them without dialing in multiple times as we develop our call flows.

Thanks to the **Browser Phone** built into OpenVBX, this plugin will let us test our flows without even touching a phone.

When you start testing, the OpenVBX Browser Phone will ring; however, once it's answered, you can continue testing the different flows or the Text-to-Speech engine while the call is ongoing.

For the plugins used in this book, I use the call flow tester heavily, so I can attest to just how handy this is to use.

Getting ready

The complete source code for this recipe can be found at `Chapter10/Recipe6` in the source code for this book.

How to do it...

We've built our plugins; now we want to test whether they work properly. This interface will let us test our call flows to make sure they all behave correctly, without using any minutes from our Twilio accounts. Perform the following steps to do so:

1. Inside your `plugins` folder, create a folder and name it `test`.

2. Upload a file called `plugin.json` bearing the following code:

```json
{
    "name" : "Call Flow Test",
    "description" : "Call Flow Test",
    "links" : [
        {
            "url" : "callflowtest",
            "script" : "plugin.php",
            "label" : "Test Call Flow",
            "menu" : "admin"
        }
    ]
}
```

3. Upload a file called `plugin.php`, bearing the following code:

```php
<?php
    $pluginData = OpenVBX::$currentPlugin->getInfo();
    require_once $pluginData['plugin_path'] . '/Test.class.php';
    $test = new Test(OpenVBX::$currentPlugin);
    $exception = false;
    if(isset($_POST['callsid'])){
      $test->setCallSid($_POST['callsid']);
    }
    try{
        if(isset($_POST['test']) AND array_key_exists($_POST['flow'],
$test->getFlows())){
          $test->callFlow($_POST['flow']);
        }
    } catch (Exception $exception) {
    }
?>
<div class="vbx-plugin">
<?php if( $exception ){?>
  <div class="notify">
    <p class="message">Could not call your OpenVBX Browser Phone -
is it online?<a href class="close action"></a></p>
  </div>
```

```php
<?php }?>
<?php if( $test->getCallSid() ){?>
  <div class="notify">
    <p class="message">Connected to the OpenVBX Browser Phone.
You can continue to test without hanging up.<a href class="close
action"></a></p>
  </div>
<?php }?>
  <h2>Test Call Flows</h2>
  <p></p>
  <p>Select a call flow to test using the OpenVBX Browser Phone
<small>Please make sure you have set your browser phone to online
first</small>:</p>
  <form action="" method="post">
    <?php echo form_dropdown('flow', $test->getFlows()) ?>
    <button class="submit-button ui-state-focus" type="submit"
name="test"><span>Test Flow</span></button>
    <input type="hidden" name="callsid" value="<?php echo $test-
>getCallSid()?>">
  </form>
</div>
```

4. Upload a file called `Tester.class.php` with the following code:

```php
<?php
class Test{
  protected $callSid;
  protected $plugin;
  public function __construct($plugin){
    $this->setPlugin($plugin);
    $this->getCI()->load->helper('form');
    $this->getCI()->load->helper('url');
  }
  public function callFlow($flow){
    $twiml = new Response();
    $twiml->addPause();
    $twiml->addRedirect( site_url('twiml/applet/voice/' . $flow
.'/start') );
    $this->startClientCall($twiml);
  }
  protected function Echo($twiml){
    return "http://twimlets.com/echo?Twiml=" . $twiml-
>asURL(true);
  }
  protected function attemptRedirect($twiml){
    if( !$this->getCallSid() ){
```

```
      return false;
    }
    $response = $this->getTwilio()->request("Accounts/".$this-
>getCI()->twilio_sid."/Calls/" . $this->getCallSid(), "GET");
    if( $response->IsError ){
      return false;
    }
    if$response->ResponseXml->Call->Status != "in-progress" ){
      return false;
    }
    $response = $this->getTwilio()->request("Accounts/".$this-
>getCI()->twilio_sid."/Calls/" . $this->getCallSid(),
"POST",array("Url" => $this->Echo($twiml)));
    if( $response->IsError ){
      return false;
    }
    if($response->ResponseXml->Call->Status != "in-progress" ){
      return false;
    }
    return true;
  }
  protected function startClientCall($twiml){
    if( $this->attemptRedirect($twiml) ){
      return;
    }
    $response = $this->getTwilio()->request(
      "Accounts/".$this->getCI()->twilio_sid."/Calls",
      "POST",
      array("Caller" => $this->getClient(),
        "To" => $this->getClient(),
        "Url" => $this->Echo($twiml)
      )
    );
    if( $response->IsError ){
      throw new Exception('error starting call');
    }
    $this->callSid = (string) $response->ResponseXml->Call->Sid;
  }
  public function getClient(){
    $client = false;
    foreach(OpenVBX::getCurrentUser()->devices as $device){
      if( 'client:' == substr($device->value, 0,
strlen('client:')) ){
        $client = $device->value;
        break;
```

```
        }
      }
      if(!$client){
        throw new Exception('could not find client');
      }
      return $client;
    }
    public function getFlows(){
      $flows = array();
      foreach(OpenVBX::getFlows() as $flow){
        $flows[ $flow->values['id'] ] = $flow->values['name'];
      }
      return $flows;
    }
    public function setCallSid($sid){
      $this->callSid = $sid;
    }
    public function getCallSid(){
      return $this->callSid;
    }
    public function getPluginInfo($key){
      $info = $this->getPlugin()->getInfo();
      return $info[$key];
    }
    public function getPlugin (){
      return $this->plugin;
    }
    public function setPlugin (Plugin $plugin){
      $this->plugin = $plugin;
    }
    public function getCI (){
      if( empty($this->ci) ){
        $this->setCI(CI_Base::get_instance());
      }
      return $this->ci;
    }
    public function setCI (CI_Base $ci){
      $this->ci = $ci;
    }
    public function getTwilio (){
      if( empty($this->twilio) ){
        $this->setTwilio( new TwilioRestClient($this->getCI()-
>twilio_sid, $this->getCI()->twilio_token) );
      }
```

```
        return $this->twilio;
    }
    public function setTwilio ($twilio){
        $this->twilio = $twilio;
    }
}
```

How it works...

In step 1, we created a folder named `test`. In step 2, we uploaded `plugin.json`.

In step 3, we created `plugin.php`, the main interface people see.

Finally, in step 4, we created `Tester.class.php`, the brain of our flow-testing plugin.

We now have a menu option under the **Admin** menu called **Test Call Flow**. This menu option will load the `plugin.php` file and will let us choose a call flow to test.

When we select a call flow to test and hit the **Test** button, we will see the Browser Phone pop up with an incoming call. This is the start of our test.

After you accept the incoming call, you will be presented with actions based on the call flow you selected.

For example, if you were testing a call flow that used the directory, it would ask you to enter a name to search for and you could test it without actually making a phone call.

Index

Thank you for buying
Twilio Cookbook

About Packt Publishing

Packt, pronounced 'packed', published its first book "*Mastering phpMyAdmin for Effective MySQL Management*" in April 2004 and subsequently continued to specialize in publishing highly focused books on specific technologies and solutions.

Our books and publications share the experiences of your fellow IT professionals in adapting and customizing today's systems, applications, and frameworks. Our solution based books give you the knowledge and power to customize the software and technologies you're using to get the job done. Packt books are more specific and less general than the IT books you have seen in the past. Our unique business model allows us to bring you more focused information, giving you more of what you need to know, and less of what you don't.

Packt is a modern, yet unique publishing company, which focuses on producing quality, cutting-edge books for communities of developers, administrators, and newbies alike. For more information, please visit our website: www.packtpub.com.

Writing for Packt

We welcome all inquiries from people who are interested in authoring. Book proposals should be sent to author@packtpub.com. If your book idea is still at an early stage and you would like to discuss it first before writing a formal book proposal, contact us; one of our commissioning editors will get in touch with you.

We're not just looking for published authors; if you have strong technical skills but no writing experience, our experienced editors can help you develop a writing career, or simply get some additional reward for your expertise.

FreeSWITCH Cookbook

ISBN: 978-1-84951-540-5   Paperback: 150 pages

Over 40 recipes to help you get the most out of your
FreeSWITCH server

1. Get powerful FreeSWITCH features to work for you

2. Route calls and handle call detailing records

3. Written by members of the FreeSWITCH
   development team

Microsoft Lync 2013 Unified Communications: From Telephony to Real-time Communication in the Digital Age

ISBN: 978-1-84968-506-1   Paperback: 224 pages

Complete coverage of all topics for a unified
communications strategy

1. A real business case and example project showing
   you how you can optimize costs and improve
   your competitive advantage with a Unified
   Communications project

2. The book combines both business and the latest
   relevant technical information so it is a great
   reference for business stakeholders, IT decision
   makers, and UC technical experts

Please check **www.PacktPub.com** for information on our titles

FreeSWITCH 1.2

ISBN: 978-1-78216-100-4   Paperback: 428 pages

Build robust, high-performance telephony systems using FreeSWITCH

1. Learn how to install and configure a complete telephony system of your own, even if this is your first time using FreeSWITCH

2. In-depth discussions of important concepts like the dialplan, user directory, NAT handling, and the powerful FreeSWITCH event socket

3. Best practices and expert tips from the FreeSWITCH experts, including the creator of FreeSWITCH, Anthony Minessale

IBM Lotus Sametime 8 Essentials: A User's Guide

ISBN: 978-1-84968-060-8   Paperback: 284 pages

Mastering Online Enterprise Communication with this collaborative software

1. Collaborate securely with your colleagues and teammates both inside and outside your organization by using Sametime features such as instant messaging and online meetings

2. Make your instant messaging communication more interesting with the inclusion of graphics, images, and emoticons to convey more information in fewer words

Please check **www.PacktPub.com** for information on our titles

CPSIA information can be obtained at www.ICGtesting.com
Printed in the USA
LVOW05s1831060913

351199LV00005B/13/P